PRAISE FOR *From Bagels to Curry*

"I highly recommend *From Bagels to Curry*. It weaves together two different worlds by showing the underlying unity. In the process, the reader gains a deeper understanding of the human heart. In *From Bagels to Curry*, Ms. Devi's Jewish family and yogic community are blended together in a delightful way. It is a little like wandering into a slightly bizarre delicatessen with bagels and lox interspersed with curries and samosas."

> – **Nayaswami Jyotish Novak**, author, including *Meditation Therapy*, and spiritual director of Ananda Village

"*From Bagels to Curry* is a gem of a book that is destined to help this weird and wonderful world we live in. A story of love and acceptance of others' faiths and cultures of which there is such a dearth in our society. In a week where we have planes being shot out of the sky and revolution and terrorism, we need simple stories like this of trust and love between all people worldwide."

> – **J Michael Fields**, author of *Nature Feels and Nature Heals* and CEO of Inspirations International

"If you've ever experienced the joy and sorrow, the laughter and tears brought about through the enduring love of family, this book is for you. Though it tells the true story of a particular family, it is an experience that we all share. Beautifully written, sensitive, and perceptive, this book was a joy to read. Don't miss it!"

> – **Nayaswami Devi Novak**, author, including *Faith Is My Armor*, and spiritual director of Ananda Village

"Drop by drop, Lila distills the essence of her relationship with her father and her path to find her place between tradition and her life's call. A story of care, differences, doubts, but above all, love."

> – **Charlotte Dufour**, author of *Land of Eternal Hope*

"A heartfelt tribute by a devoted but independent daughter to her remarkable father, *From Bagels to Curry* is at the same time a story of how alternative spiritual paths have affected families of traditional religions—in this case, Judaism. In the end, the old adage proves true: love conquers all."

> — **Richard Salva**, author, including *Walking with William of Normandy*

"The power of Yogananda's teaching shines through Ms. Devi's personal story, gently expanding our horizons. Most of all, an undercurrent of love is felt throughout her book, which is the highest teaching life has to offer. As she writes: 'When all is said and done, what endures is the love.'"

> — **Jayadev Jaerschky**, author, including *Respira Che Ti Passa*, and yoga and meditation teacher

"Approaching death, as described in this book, is always a time when superficialities are stripped away and shared humanity comes forward. The story of the passing of a dynamic and much loved father of five children is uplifting, instructive, and entertaining as we get to know the father and the family through the eyes of his only daughter."

> — **Asha Praver**, author, including *Loved and Protected*, and spiritual director of Ananda, Palo Alto

"Funny and sweet, poignant and profound. As the lives of a father and daughter entwine in the final chapters of his life, the author illumines a story of love's redeeming power. Traversing the territory of the Soul in its quest for freedom, *From Bagels to Curry* shines with inspiration that will touch us all."

> — **Dana Lynn Andersen**, Founder of Awakening Arts Academy

"Lila Devi has done a masterful job with a very tricky subject. How does an author reveal the process of stepping out of her regular life into the role of primary caregiver during her father's last months, especially given his larger-than-life Jewish influence on everyone around him? Yet she does it beautifully, gracefully, and never with self-pity or sadness. This book is impactful and triumphant--a loving tribute to a man, who no one (and you, the reader) will soon forget."

> – **Savitri Simpson**, lecturer and author, including *Through Many Lives* and *Chakras for Starters*

"Ms. Devi weaves spiritual insights into her relationships with her father and family. This read is filled with wisdom, humor and compassion."

> – **Diksha McCord**, author, including *Global Kitchen*

"This is a wonderful inspiring book! Spiritually uplifting, and not lacking humour, Lila Devi has interestingly covered 'the mystery of life, death, family, and freedom' in this simple and fascinating tale of her father and her own spiritual awakening and journey to finding true joy and freedom."

> – **Stephen Sturgess**, author, including *The Yoga Book*

"An honest-to-God account of the beginnings of the author's spiritual quest, reminiscent of a Socratic apology and equally convincing and moving. She refreshingly flouts normal literary conventions, making her varied and pacey narrative a joy to read."

> – **David Connolly**, Professor of Literary Translation and author, including *Deadline In Athens*

PRAISE FOR *From Bagels to Curry* BY THE AUTHOR'S BROTHERS
(IN ORDER OF DESCENDING AGE)

"In this totally insightful book, my sister uncovers the essence of our father's zest for life and the unwavering strength with which he struggled through to the end of his life here on earth."
— **Phillip Zaret**, Physician

"Our sister writes with an unprecedented and infectiously inspiring viewpoint about our loving though sometimes chaotic upbringing. With a Jewish-flavored secularism, our father osmotically taught us to make others feel welcome; that life is beautiful; that time is not meant to be wasted; and above all that nothing is more important than family. He had a dancer's passion for life! This book will take you on just such a dance."
— **Jack Zaret**, Consultant

"*From Bagels to Curry* captures the struggles for purpose and meaning in life as my father approached his passing. His challenge in maintaining his dignity when confronted with inevitable death became an amazing legacy handed to the children he loved so much."
— **Moshe Dovid Zaret**, Rabbi

"*From Bagels to Curry* is a truly inspirational story of our father's handling of his impending death from the time of his diagnosis of pancreatic cancer through the end of his days. He lived with an unwavering positive attitude and zest for life. In his deep hazel eyes, the glass was ALWAYS half full. This special outlook on life never wavered from the time of his fatal diagnosis through his last breath. Thanks, Sis, for writing such a wonderful story!"
— **Thomas C. Zaret**, Attorney at Law

FROM BAGELS TO CURRY

*Life, Death,
Family, and Triumph*

LILA DEVI

Other Books by the Author

The Essential Flower Essence Handbook
(also in Italian, Japanese, Czech, Romanian, and English in India)

Flower Essences for Animals
(also in Japanese)

Bradley Banana and The Jolly Good Pirate
(also in Italian and Romanian—the first published children's picture book in a series of 20)

FROM BAGELS TO CURRY

*Life, Death,
Family, and Triumph*

LILA DEVI

crystal clarity **publishers**
Nevada City, CA 95959

Crystal Clarity Publishers, Nevada City, CA 95959

Copyright ©2015 by Lila Devi
All Rights Reserved. Published 2015

Printed in the United States of America

ISBN-13: 978-1-56589-297-2
eISBN-13: 978-1-56589-558-4

Library of Congress Cataloging-in-Publication Data Available

Book Cover Design by Martin Wolfe
Back Cover Photo by Gennadjy Andreev

www.crystalclarity.com
clarity@crystalclarity.com
800-424-1055

Dedicated to:

My beloved outrageous father,

and those who would follow
their hearts to their chosen path.

I will lift up mine eyes unto the hills
From whence cometh my help.
My help cometh from the Lord,
Who made the heavens and the earth.
—Psalm 121:1-2

He who beholds Me everywhere,
And who beholds everything in Me,
Never loses sight of Me;
Nor do I lose sight of him.
—Bhagavad Gita 6:30

ACKNOWLEDGEMENTS

My deepest gratitude goes to: My family and relatives for contributing in so many ways to this book: my brothers and their wives, children, and grandchildren; Jackie Sunshine; my father's friends and neighbors; my spiritual family of many decades and countries; Jim Prakash Van Cleave, Lakshman Heubert, Bob Yehling, and Savitri Simpson, whose wisdom has added to these pages a rich coating of editorial polish. Linda Schwartz, who supported my plan to turn my journal into a book; Tejindra Scott Tully, for helping to brainstorm the title; Martin Wolfe who captured the text's life force in the cover design; David Jensen, for sculpting the perfect fonts in the typeset; Skip Gurudas Barrett and Crystal Clarity Publishers for his/their encouragement and support; my nursing angel Sharon Taylor who offered her words and her friendship without fail no matter when I phoned; the hospice and health care workers who gave so valiantly of their hearts; my mother, whose love is always with me; my father, a *mensch* among *mensches*, for never once letting me beat him in checkers; my best friend and spiritual guide, Swami Kriyananda; my Guru, Paramhansa Yogananda, in silent grace.

Names have been changed to protect privacy except for close family members and friends.

Contents

WALKING OFF TO HEAVEN

Dad and grandson Noah, August, 2008

Recently brother Tommy said,
"Dad's an easy guy to miss. Noah talks about him all the time.
Rather than spending his last days mentally dulled
by medication, Dad chose the pain of his illness in order
to maintain a truer awareness.
He wanted whatever life he could hold onto."

Tommy took this photo on his cell phone
two weeks before Dad died, saying:
"It looked like Dad was holding Noah's hand
and walking off to Heaven."

FOREWORD

This is one of those books that gives away the ending fairly quickly—in fact, in the title's byline. It's neither a whodunit nor a gripping thriller with perilous twists of theme and plot but rather a simple tale of the stunning mystery of life, death, family, and triumph. As you will see, Dad was such an amazing character that it would have been impossible *not* to write this book.

Aaron Oscar (Zeke) Zaret passed from this world on September 14, 2008, eight days shy of his eighty-first birthday after a five-and-a-half-month battle with pancreatic cancer. Truly he was in the prime of his life with more songs to sing, dances to dance, stories to tell. As unwilling as Dad was to leave this world, his sojourn on earth seemed to have reached its completion. His skills as a surgical supply salesman ensured that his telephone calls were always succinct—professional yet courteous, friendly though not chatty. He was never one to overstay his welcome, neither on the telephone nor in this world.

My decision to join a yoga community could have had the power to tear our family apart much like *kariya*, the symbolic tearing of clothing of the mourners at an orthodox funeral. Somehow it didn't. When all is said and done, what endures is the love. Isn't it so that people tend to remain their parents' children no matter what their age? This is true of my four younger brothers and myself. After my mother Harriet left this world seven years before Dad, he cared for us without exception—remaining interested, engaged, and interactive in our lives. He left each of us with many endearing memories of our times together. As I sat at his bedside a few weeks before his passing, savoring those moments when daylight hovers on a thinning horizon before disappearing into paler shades, I said to him, "Dad, you'll be my father for the rest of your life."

"No," he corrected me with slow and deliberate speech. "I'll be your father for the rest of *your* life."

From Bagels to Curry first began as a journal written during Dad's last days. It has since grown to something more universal—beyond a comfort for my family and a healing process for me. Even as he hoped to immortalize his life by telling his tales, I wanted to do the same by recording his words. I also wrote this book for my brothers. At the unveiling ceremony of Dad's gravestone six months after his death, I handed each of them a plastic-bound hard-copy version. This book is "rated G for grandchildren" so that Dad in the role of Jewish grandfather, or Zayde, can be known by his children's children and on into future generations.

The original journal preface reads:

Until his last breath, Dad remained a father, grandfather, great-grandfather, husband, partner, brother, son, uncle, cousin, friend, neighbor, salesman, singer, dancer, storyteller, humorist, artist, card and Scrabble player, restaurant patron, tennis player, sports enthusiast, and all-round lover of life. Enclosed here are threads of those last days with our father—the times he laughed, struggled, and overcame. But most of all, the times he loved and was loved in return. His passing was courageous, valiant, victorious. May these words help your heart to heal from loss and be filled with the joy of his spirit. To my brothers and their families, to my mother and, after her passing, his girlfriend Jackson: Please enjoy this compilation of treasured times with Dad. My hope is that in some small way this journal will give you a part of him as you knew and loved him, and know and love him still. It was written in loving service to Dad. May he live in our hearts forever.

My father was his own best story. He was the epitome of outrageousness; in fact, he could have patented it, distilled it, and made a small fortune from it as well. Often the finest dramas are the ones that do not proceed with saccharine smoothness—but rather those filled with conflict, challenge, and hard-won victory, much like the rocky drama of our father-daughter relationship.

Oddly enough, Dad and I were perfectly suited to each other. I wasn't the boy-child he'd hoped for, nor was he the doting father I craved. This made us an ideal match. Through the rite of passage of birth, we enter this world from a higher, more spiritually refined realm. Call it Heaven or the astral world. My innate mistake lay in assuming that heavenly harmony would continue— which through Dad it didn't. I landed in this world expecting a fairy-tale father. He wasn't. In truth, all I had to do was come to a better understanding of this person who played his part so well. I caught a glimpse of that higher reality in his last days. As you are about to discover within these pages, my father's biography is interspersed with tidbits of my own life—and fittingly so, since the life of a parent is by nature entwined with those of his children.

Some years after graduating from the University of Michigan, I reconnected with a former college friend. "You struck me as someone who was always looking for something," he said. My friend was right. I eventually found that "something" in my spiritual path. A copy of Paramhansa Yogananda's spiritual classic *Autobiography of A Yogi* caught my eye at a neighbor's home. So deeply did the author's photo imprint itself into my consciousness that a few weeks later I read the book. Unable to put it down until I'd finished it cover to cover, I lay reading on rock outcroppings in the sketchy sunlight of northwestern Montana where my meager earthly dreams had reached their fruition in a free-form back-to-the land lifestyle. I was in my early twenties. This work, I recognized instantly, held the key to what I'd been seeking. In so many words, Yogananda described his mission: to bring to the world a new dispensation in the purest forms of original yoga and original Christianity.

Less than a year later in December of 1976, I made my way to the intentional community of Ananda Village in Northern California, comprised of like-minded people who followed the teachings of Yogananda. Ananda was founded in 1968. With its branch colonies and meditation groups scattered across the globe, it has become one of the most successful communities of its kind in the world today. Yogananda answered my own heart's calling in his mission statement: to "spread a spirit of brotherhood among all peoples, and aid in establishing, in many countries, self-sustaining world brotherhood colonies for plain living and high thinking."

The founder of Ananda, J. Donald Walters (1926-2013), was Yogananda's direct disciple. Swami Kriyananda, or Swamiji as we called him, lived with the great Indian master at his Los Angeles headquarters for the last three and a half years of Yogananda's life. I can say with inner certainty that Swami quickly became, and has remained throughout my life, my guiding light and best friend, even after his recent passing.

My father went to his grave convinced that Ananda had taken advantage of me. Whereas I felt I'd reached a zenith in my yet-green life, he remained certain that I'd sought out Ananda from a sense of need, only to be warmly welcomed and then insidiously robbed—of both my identity and my money.

Instead I felt I'd attained the peak of my fulfilled desires—though not exactly what one would call worldly goals. I'd worked as a kindergarten teacher's aide for the children of cattle ranchers who finished their nap time with the comfort of their thumbs in their mouths. I lived off the land as one did back in the hippie era, ate organically from the garden, and ground my own flour to bake many dozens of loaves of bread in a stove heated with firewood that I'd split with my own hands until they blistered and calloused over. My companions included a fine circle of spiritual friends and a small herd of milk goats. Often I'd fumble through the basics of meditation once the evening chores were completed. After securing the goats in the barn for their milking, I would rest my head against the flanks of my capricious livestock, the warm white liquid with its goaty scent clacking rhythmically into the stainless steel bucket.

It was hard to imagine life could get any better.

With a rolled-up sleeping bag strapped to my backpack and a handmade dulcimer under my arm, I arrived at Ananda Village. I'd either be gone a week, I told my backwoods friends with no uncertain drama, or forever. It's beginning to look like forever.

My parents were not merely heartbroken by my decision to move to a "cult." They were devastated. By leaving Judaism, they felt I'd betrayed their ideals. Yet as the years passed, my mother warmed to my lifestyle choice. Judaic tradition says it's one thing to be born a Gentile—these anomalies simply happen—but quite another to be born "one of the chosen" into what Judaism considers the only true religion. And then to *leave* it?

Jewish law would say I'm still Jewish. So does my own heart. To this day I hold dear the memories of my upbringing, even though in many ways our home was only peripherally religious. We were neither orthodox nor conservative nor reform. We were, simply, Jewish. I cherish to this day the memories of the deep love of family, the devotion and prayer, the God-reminding significance of the holy holidays, and the honoring of the many traditions that mark the Jewish calendar year.

My decision to step away from Judaism and thus from my birth family was both agonizing and liberating. That my parents were so self-blaming about my choice didn't make it any easier! As their firstborn, I was the child on whom they felt they'd made the most mistakes. *Oy vey*, they would say, *if only we'd raised her better, this NEVER would have happened!* Leaving the active practice of Judaism was a confusing but necessary step in my evolution, as though in so doing I was somehow "not right in the head." *If I couldn't find Hashem in the religion into which I'd been born, where* did *I expect to find Him?* Add to this the subliminal pressure: "How could you *do* such a thing?" Or even less subliminal: "How could you do this to *us?*" Contemplation of the fifth of the Ten Commandments gave me cause to reflect: "Thou shalt honor thy father and mother."

Yet what exactly does "honor" mean?

Like most children, of *course* I wanted to please and not disappoint my parents. But at what cost? Where does one draw the line? What is a child's responsibility to his progenitors, and do they want to see the fulfillment of their offspring's dreams—or their own? By following what I believed to be my true calling, was I not honoring them in the highest possible way? Ancient yogic scripture promises that one who finds God blesses his family both before and after his own life for seven generational incarnations.

Indeed most parents want the best for their children. Yet problems can arise when they assume they know what "best" means. Parental love by its nature is well-intentioned. Even so, how often does that love contain undercurrents difficult for the child-turned-adult to break away from? *I'll love you if you behave a certain way. I'll love you if you live your life according to my wishes. And I will love you forever if you make me proud.*

For all my father's dearness, I saw again and again that his children's successes were measured by what made him the most proud. Not that I fault him for his attitudes. The yogic doctrine of karma and reincarnation has helped me to understand that I chose *him* as my father, not the other way around—nor by some random cosmic coincidence, the tenets of karma being too vast to delve into here. I must say that the tensions between us caused by my not actively practicing Judaism are only now after his passing beginning to dissolve.

One point that becomes clearer to me with the passing of time is that my choice of this family was ideal. My desire for a perfect childhood in some ways affirmed my resistance to the very people I'd deliberately drawn into my life. Acknowledging the divine perfection of our bond in the last days of my father's life was a great blessing. Indeed, his courage to face his death helped me to cultivate the stamina to write this book.

I sometimes ask myself how I happened to land in this family with these souls. My wonderment remains unresolved to the point of sometimes questioning, who *are* these people? My younger brothers—with whose lives my own entwines like a tapestry in parts colorful and fluid, in others knotty and unraveled—are listed here in order of descending age. In the spirit of the Old Testament that begins with who begat whom, these are the "begats" of our family.

In Philip David, my father had the boy child he wanted. Dad's oldest son is a handsome man named after his own father who left this world many decades past, Jewish tradition decreeing a newborn be named after the deceased, not the living. Phil became a doctor, an osteopath, the profession that Dad had deeply desired for himself; but it remained unobtainable due to the harsh circumstances of his early life. My brother and his wife Patty have three children: Olivia, Emily, and Zachary. Dad sparkled when Phil called and visited. He loved what Phil has accomplished in his life and bragged about him unceasingly.

Jack Leslie too made his father proud. As the senior sales coordinator for a large dot-com, Jackie absorbed his father's ability to connect with people, along with his mother's gift to see deeply into life's subtleties and articulate them poetically. Jackie has the heart of an artist.

Daniel Michael, who became the orthodox Moshe Dovid, sensed his life's calling when barely into his teens. Dad practically doubled in size when bragging about his-son-the-rabbi. He and Bracha have blessed Zayde with four grandchildren: Devorah Leebah, Shmuel, Chana, and Sara. Leeby and her husband Akiva gave Zayde his first great-grandchildren: Yehuda, Chaim, Chaya, and—several months after Dad passed—a boy named after my father, followed by other children.

Thomas Cary shares with Dad the role of youngest in a large family. According to my father, we weren't complete without a lawyer to form the perfect Jewish home: the doctor, the lawyer, the rabbi, and the Indian chief. Tommy and Liz have three children: Perri, Tess, and Noah. How proudly Dad asked his youngest son when the need arose for legal advice!

Then there's me, his firstborn and only daughter. Whereas my brothers were supposed to become successful doctors, lawyers, and rabbis, I was supposed to marry one. They did what was expected of them. I didn't. Oh, on occasion he bragged about me too. But to one of the hospice aides once his illness progressed, he mentioned only his sons.

"Say, Dad?" I cleared my throat though it didn't need clearing. "What about me?"

"Yes," he said by way of introduction, "this is my-daughter-the-midget."

It is with great joy that I now introduce you to Dad and to this book. (Please refer to the glossaries of Jewish and yogic words and phrases placed at the back of the book in order to avoid the formality of too many footnotes.) Perhaps you too have a father, a close relative, or a loved one who has passed on or is nearing transition. Maybe you are struggling to smooth out the gruff edges of a less-than-ideal parental relationship or have set out on your own, leaving behind a time-honored familial tradition, religion, or culture to follow your own path to truth. Sometimes we learn about love in ways that test us greatly—that we think are beyond our ability to endure but ultimately bring us to a glorious place within our own heart's vastness. Such was the glad resolution I found with my father. *From Bagels to Curry* is his story, and his daughter's. It's my song, my dance, my offering to you.

On your own perfect journey, may you find the joy within you.

My Father's Smile

The hot sun burrows into the cracked pavement of Chicago's slum district as a young boy weaves between pickups and cars of the mid-Thirties: Flathead V8-engine Ford Coupes and Sedans, Chevys, Buicks, Cadillacs, and an occasional Bugatti making its way to more upscale neighborhoods. With eight years to his name and as many coins in his pocket, Aaron is already honing the skills of an astute salesman that will someday help him provide for a wife and five kids. The boy flashes a perfect smile. Getting down to business, he rolls up the sleeves of his threadbare shirt with button holes that outnumber its buttons— though no buttons ever seem to be missing.

Keeping time with the predictable thump of a poorly syncopated two-step, the wagon cart careens from side to side, heaving a sigh beneath its cargo of frosty soda pop cartons. Wheels squeak and bottles clank. There are no coolers, no refrigerators, no soda machines to chill the drinks. Aaron buys several bags of ice while people all around him melt into the heat in a frothy slow motion. Nothing beats a frosty drink in the scorching squalor. Everyone loves the sodas.

What a treasure on the grimy Windy City afternoons!

To keep food on their table, Aaron's parents brainstorm the business idea while across the nation banks fail and stocks crash, riveting into the black hole of The Great Depression. The global woes preceding the next World War are barely half-spent. At twenty-four bottles to a case, the boy's mother and father buy the sodas at two cents each. Aaron vendors them at five cents a bottle. A single Sunday might earn them a hefty ten dollars in loose change that clatters like the thick-necked bottles, with the sale of as many as twenty cases.

Life's rhythms, full of possibilities and promises, sprawl before the young boy like a board game with new moves, clever strategies, and endless challenges. He will tackle them all in the years to come without missing a beat.

I can almost hear the squeaky wheels on the blistering pavement and see the bottles bobbing in the melting ice water. I can see Aaron's big smile as he sells his wares to the grateful patrons, his shirt pasted with dampness across the bony hollow of his chest.

"That was a lotta money back then," Dad says with a grin.

Forever in my heart is burrowed my father's smile.

THE HEART OF A PATRIARCH

Dad passed.

We began the Jewish custom of sitting *shiva*. All five of Aaron's children sat on sofas and chairs, their cushions removed to symbolize the mourning that devoured our five hearts.

Okay, so we were also giggling and joking ourselves silly. We laughed so hard that we couldn't stop even if we tried. At what, we couldn't say, nor did it matter in the way that the enigmatic catharsis of grief picks you up by the shoulders and drops you outside the boundaries of your everyday life. With the same freedom of leaning to the left at the Passover table, we mourners could behave carte blanche any way we pleased. Dad was free, and his victory gave us cause to rejoice. His suffering in this world had ended with the finality of a novel read from cover to cover and definitively slammed shut to take its place between other dusty books with their rough-hewn bindings that rested on aged wooden bookshelves—now and forever, upright and forgotten.

According to our family custom, each of Aaron's sons spoke, always in order of descending age as was our tradition for group photographs and now for our father's *shiva*.

Phil: "Dad was a provider. He made us feel safe. There were no worries about food or clothing. He took care of us. We came first, Mom was next, and he was always last. He did whatever he had to do to put food on the table.

"I look around and see Dad everywhere. I'm happy to have Mom and Dad together."

Jackie: "I had a hard time knowing we'd gather for this event. I never wanted to know what this feels like but we kids have to go through it.

"Dad loved all people. I love how Dad included everyone. He made all our friends feel like a part of our family, he never wanted anyone to feel left out. Dad was always sharing. Look around at us five kids. We either look like him or we joke like him!

"It was so hard to see him go and to such a hard cancer. All the way to the end, his mind was so incredibly sharp. It just shows you the power of the human spirit. He was so brave that till the end he thought he could beat it.

"When you're a little boy, you want to think your father is Superman. I did, and Dad was. We were once little kids like you (pointing at Zayde's grandchildren). Time goes by so quickly. When Zayde said, 'Do a good job,' he meant we were brought up to make the world a better place. He will be wonderfully judged by Hashem."

Moshe: "I remember being seven years old and walking downtown with Dad. Toward us walks a beggar.

"'You have such a nice son,' the ragged man says, resting his hand on my shoulder. 'Can you spare a quarter?'

"Dad sensed my fear and the first thing he says is, 'Please take your hand off my son.' The moral is that when you were around Dad, you felt safe.

"I also remember shopping with him at Hudson's Department Store at the Northland Mall in Detroit. We happened to bump into a doctor who knew Dad. 'You need to know,' he tells me, 'I got advice from your dad. Every piece of advice I listened to, I profited. Every piece I didn't listen to, I lost out.' In those words. Dad was so good at what he did. He knew his job inside out like nobody's business.

Tommy: "Dad was always kind to strangers. Once when Mom was having a hard time—she needed a lot of home care that was practically round the clock for him—a delivery boy with a carry-out dinner knocked at the door. You never knew Dad had any stress. He was gracious to everyone he was in touch with, even when ninety-nine out of a hundred people were not in a good mood. Always he was thinking of others."

Several close relatives added their recollections.

Shmuel, Zayde's oldest grandson: "I remember the time Zayde's neighbor Louisa came to visit him when his illness had advanced. The first and only thing he said to her even with no energy was, 'You look beautiful.'

"My Zayde always wanted to know waiters and waitresses by name. He made them feel like people, not servants.

"'Do you have any fear?' I asked Zayde toward the end of his life.

"'I've not been afraid of living,' he said, 'and so I'm not afraid of dying.'"

Chana, Shmuel's sister: "He had such a joy of life. He appreciated everything! I used to ask him, 'Zayde, why are you always singing?'

"'Hashem is so good to me,' he said. I could list the things that *weren't* wonderful about him because it would be shorter. He always looked at the good, and that's why he was such a happy person. He remembered people's names. I'd forget but Zayde, he remembered, even when we'd return to a restaurant weeks later. He respected and cared about everyone."

Moshe's wife Bracha: "Your mom and dad flew out to Jerusalem for the first Passover after I married their rabbi son. One day in the kitchen, I accidentally dropped the blender and it shattered on the tile floor. Your father, *oy*. He walked around the streets of Jerusalem not knowing how to speak Hebrew, and somehow he came home with a blender! When he put his mind to something, he did it.

"Two days after Shmuel was born—that was two days before the *bris*—your mom saw he was sick. So they took him to the hospital and admitted him for six days. We suspected Shmuel had meningitis. It was very serious. Dad took the shift from midnight to six in the morning so his first grandson would never be alone in the hospital and without family. Surely no one understood this better than Dad as the youngest of seven children, since he himself had never been alone! He just did whatever it took. He never complained."

Then Moshe spoke again. "Dad made living easier for everyone. He was happy with his lot in life."

"When his condo was closing, I had to go pick up his mail that his neighbor Maria was holding. She says to me, 'I miss your Dad so much.'

"*Nu*, so I asked, 'What do you miss about him?'

"She said, 'When he came into the complex, he would be whistling and humming. Sometimes he would dance for me.'

"A *simchas hachayim*, what a joy of life he expressed! Every one of us has had challenging times as Dad has. Life is difficult, it's a big challenge. Dad was such an example of right attitude—that if you can't be happy going through life, it's not worth it. He owned that joy, that positive approach and an appreciation of whatever he had because he grew up with so little. Maria misses Dad and his amazing nature. He had a contagious happiness."

Tommy: "Dad was a glowing beam of light. How happy, how joyous he was, and he didn't get upset over little things! Jackie told him recently about a billionaire who took his own life, even though he left this world with billions of dollars. Dad didn't have a lot materially, but he was the wealthiest person I've ever known because of his outlook on life. He was the richest guy, ever. His family meant everything to him. He was about making everyone feel special."

Tom's wife Liz: "I'm also sharing for my children who are too shy to talk right now. Zayde was accepting of people and their particular personalities. Whenever he visited us, he was chatty if we wanted to talk and silent if we didn't. It was always about the other person's comfort. He had a special bond with each of our kids, a connection without words."

"Okay everybody, listen up," five-year-old Noah chimed in, momentarily overstepping the chasm of his shyness. "My Zayde— he taught me how to twirl my spaghetti."

CANCER-SCHMANCER

The diagnostic tests all indicate something serious, something that explains why my father's body is "closing up shop." Dad and his girlfriend Jackson missed a red-eye flight to the Bahamas. Instead he was hospitalized. Little did they know a journey of a different kind was about to begin.

"I told you not to come," Dad tells me. "*Nu*, since you're here, I'm happy to see you." A proud man, he never wants to bother anyone nor does he want them to bother about him. Dad is Dad as much as ever.

The car ride from the airport to the hospital with my brother Jackie is light and connective. We stay forty-five minutes, a long time for Dad. Not one to make a *tzimmes*, he asks Moshe and family to leave after only two and a half minutes. Clearly Dad is uncomfortable being fussed over. With no little awkwardness, I place a box of chocolates and a very Jewish chicken-soup get-well card in front of him.

"I told you not to spend money," he says gruffly.

I mutter a half-truth to deflect the focus of the gift away from him. "It's for the nurses, Dad." That, he can live with. What he appreciates is that I brought him a copy of the *Los Angeles Times*.

"Thanks, Dolly, I'll read it later." The names Dad calls his first-born swish through my mental rinse cycle: Linnie, Lin, Dolly, Sweetie, Sister, Baby. Many times in the months ahead, he'll call out these names as I rush to his side—to fluff his pillows, to fetch the newspaper, to pour him bottled juice not two and not four but exactly three fingers high.

"No worries, Dad, I already cut out the puzzle on the comics page." We share a laugh and I wonder if my feigned light-heartedness sounds as transparent to him as it does to me. He reads my card attentively and stuffs it back into the envelope.

"Don't you want to leave it out so you can look at it?" I ask.

"No. It's too private." The card, I'm sensing, is very precious to him. Dad's never been one to wear his heart on his sleeve. His condominium in North Hollywood is cluttered with stacks of cards sent by loved ones over the years—birthday cards, Father's Day cards, thinking-of-you cards—but no get-well cards lurk in the shadowy piles because there's never been cause to send them. Even when he battled and recovered from prostate cancer ten years ago, we never thought of him as ill. Dad as always was just Dad.

With a brusqueness that overshadows his kindness, my father greets my return to his hospital room later that evening. He eats little of his dinner. Despite my prodding efforts of encouragement, he manages only a few bites.

"I feel shaky and I don't like the way I look. Linnie?" he asks. "What do you think?"

"You look strong and vital, Dad. Honest, your energy's great. Maybe you're a little pale but gosh—who wouldn't be with all the procedures here?"

"All night long the nurses wake me up to ask me if I'm sleeping. What are they, *nuts*?"

"Whatever this is, Zeke," says Dr. Ayal, "we'll take care of it and you can fight it."

The internist's optimism brings comfort. On wings of life-affirming hope, the human spirit soars with the news we all want to hear. Yet my bigger-than-life father knows exactly what's happening within him.

Certainly he'll be pleased when I hand him two photographs trimmed and framed to keep by his bedside that previously adorned his refrigerator door, held in place by an assortment of tattered magnets touting advertising slogans. The one taken less than a year ago of Dad on the sofa with his grandchildren captures the familial levity of his eightieth birthday party. The other shows us five kids and several spouses seated on the back steps of Moshe's house, clustered together like figurines on a pop-up greeting card.

"Oh *no-o*," Dad says emphatically, "put those back on the refrigerator." *What was I thinking?* Of course that's what he'd say.

"But these are your *favorites*!" My croaky voice echoes faintly off the stark paint of the hospital walls, my good intentions quashed on the sterile floor. Feeling like a cat whose tail has just been stepped on, I mentally retreat to a safe, quiet place within myself.

"I don't want to show off and make people who have less than me feel uncomfortable," my parent says.

Dad grabs the remote control, flips through the channels of the tiny television mounted on the wall near his bed, and settles comfortably into a baseball game.

It's the top of the third inning.

"Linnie, how nice you look."

I walk into the hospital room later that day and place a bird-like kiss on my father's cheek to the fanfare of a monotone voice paging doctors on the intercom. The heavy door closes vault-like behind me, trampling the disincarnate message beneath the hall-way din of shuffling feet and meal-cart wheels. The institutional air smells stuffy, old, stale in my nostrils as though it's been ex-haled by too many people and recycled well beyond its natural shelf life.

"It's nice to see you in those open-toed sandals I bought for you." Dad is in good spirits.

"And you also got me the underwear I'm wearing on one of our other shopping trips."

"I don't want to see that," he adds, joking but not smiling.

Indeed nothing seems very funny right now. We've had some fine shopping trips over the years. Appearance has always been important to my father who wore even his childhood slum rags with an air of unassuming dignity. Likewise he wants to see his children stylishly dressed. Though he often says how classy Mom was, he too has developed a polished yet simple elegance of wardrobe. Passing this refinement of dress to his children I can tell pleases him greatly.

"I'm tired now, Linda. I'd like to watch the Lakers game." Dad's attempt to hide his nervousness about tomorrow's test results sounds frail and lacking substance.

Over the coming months, all five of us children will watch many baseball, football, and tennis games with him, though we're not much into spectator sports. We'd rather be out there playing. Still, we all want quality time with our father—in whatever ways he wishes with whatever time we have left together. Dad seems stressed. Perhaps because he's processing so much inwardly that no true rest is possible?

"Actually, Dad, I'm fine with whatever happens. Trust me. I'm okay with this. You've made us all strong and we'll get through this." I'm feeling suddenly a little tipsy, oxygen-deprived, and mildly claustrophobic in the sterile room.

"It's time for you to go, Dolly," he says abruptly, clearly not wanting to engage in any deep talks. The mere thought of the looming diagnostic news not yet revealed is too raw, too fresh. Dad's loss of control over the life he loves so dearly is just beginning. I pour him a glass of water, crack open the door to the exact degree he requests—no more and no less—and leave the hospital.

It's a tense and packed day as we await the specialist's diagnosis. The results are still incomplete but preliminary tests confirm cancer of the liver. More details will be revealed at tomorrow's oncology appointment with Dr. Beckwitz.

One by one my brothers come to visit Dad.

"You know," he tells Phil, "I was only twenty years old when I lost my own father."

"That's right, Dad, we know. *Nu*, like you haven't told us a billion times before?" Phil's quick wit compels him to look for the joke hidden within every verbal banter, though he can't seem to find one here.

"And look how old *you* are," Dad says, defining his life in terms of parenting. "Now you'll have to continue your journey without me." He talks about his father dying of stomach cancer sixty years ago, not merely telling the story. He becomes it. "This is how it went," he begins, which Phil sees as his cue for a good-bye.

"Okay, Pops, gotta go." Phil rises, then turns back at the door. "You know how I got evidence that I wasn't adopted? I got your sense of humor. Just remember, Bupkies, whatever doesn't kill ya makes ya stronger. *You be good.* You too, Sis." My-brother-the-doctor exits the room before a solitary tear falls from the corner of his eye. I send him an air-kiss, visualizing him decades ago in his little cowboy hat and chaps, so proud and so vulnerable, the new sheriff in town.

Settling into a cross-legged position in the chair next to Dad's bed, I balance my arms precariously on my knees. No matter how many decades cling to my aging frame, my knees will forever remain a poor resting place for my elbows.

Aaron continues. "Our family didn't have a doctor. I was a medic in the Navy, so they want my advice: 'Should your father have surgery or not?' *Nu*, they're asking *me*?" he says rhetorically, raising his palms and his shoulders as if in a choreographed dance step. "Everyone hoped an operation would let him live longer."

"*Hmm*." I nod with feigned interest as though I hadn't heard the story a million times before. Had Dad not been so enraptured by his own delivery, I knew—as the astute judge of character he'd become through his many years of salesmanship—that he would have intuited my boredom infused with daughterly respect. Fortunately, nothing engrosses Dad more than one of his own stories about his favorite subject. *Himself*. Storytelling is how my father communicates, maintains control, and sometimes hides from making deeper connections. Not one to share his feelings outright, instead he entertains.

"I'm twenty years old at the time," Dad continues, "and what do I know? But a *shlimazel* I'm not. So I say yes to the surgery. Sure, why not?" Up go the palms and the shoulders. "My father was an angry man—so angry it's not even funny. And so furious about the cancer that he had to be confined to his hospital bed with restraints. I'll bet you the pain meds back in those days were worthless unless they were heavy opiates. I felt so guilty, so bad, that I couldn't bring myself to visit my father in the hospital."

Dad lowers his eyes, the weight of the memory no longer bearable. Never before has he mentioned the restraints to anyone.

As if by magic to break the tension, a Filipino nurse named Lina walks into the room, her steps rendered soft and inconspicuous by her thick-soled shoes. "You know, Zeke," she says, toying with the stethoscope draped around the back of her neck like a trained pet snake, "my mother-in-law is ninety-four years old. I've been taking care of her for the last thirty years."

Dad, the consummate "people person," expresses interest in her life story before shifting the spotlight of his narrative onto me. He brags about his businesswoman-entrepreneur-author daughter who travels the world. Depending on his mood at the time, his description of me might run the gamut from praise to insults. This shiftiness is one of his behaviors that over the years I've simply learned to tolerate.

The Los Angeles traffic yawns into the late afternoon while Aaron's son-the-rabbi comes to visit. Moshe strides hurriedly into the room, always busy, busy, busy, cutting a fine figure in his black suit and white shirt. The tassels of his *tzitzit* hang just below his waistline in a dance of jewelry made of linen. This symbolic Jewish custom of wearing fringes from a four-cornered garment reflects the multitude of Commandments to be ever-remembered. Moshe's trimmed graying beard offsets the black *yarmulke* sitting on the crown of his head like a languid cow in a pasture after a milking. How readily I remember that twinkle in his eyes when as a kid he'd just done something mischievous that he knew he wouldn't get caught for—and even if he did, he could always talk his way out of his own culpability.

"I'll show them what it means to fight this," Dad tells Moshe. "Be realistic." His voice rings with strength of will and driving forcefulness. "You have to be happy and think positive. I know I'm not going to beat this, but I'm going to last as long as I can."

"We know, Dad," says Moshe checking his watch, "we know you will." The rabbi settles into a metal-framed chair whose purpose is strictly functional and as devoid of comfort as it is of beauty. "So, how's by you? Tell me the whole *megillah*. I've got *shpilkes*."

"The nurses have such a hard life here working with so many sick people. When I make them laugh, I know I'm doing something worthwhile."

"That's because you're so humble."

"Humble-schmumble, whaddaya talkin' about?" Dad says in his own brand of religious rhetoric, adjusting the plastic hospital bracelet on his wrist. How easily he finds the *chutzpah* in Jewish humor, its remnants transmuted from the Jewish people's long-suffering history of persecution.

Dad tells one familial story after another to Tommy, Moshe, and me—mostly about his working career and how with five young kids to feed, my mother's father Grampa Levine refused his request for financial help for the schooling to become a doctor.

"I paid for Phil's medical school and Tommy's law school."

"Then why," I ask, as I had many times before without receiving a satisfying answer, "did I have to put myself through college?"

"It was Mom's idea." My father's quickest responses are the ones I trust the least. "We were still following 'the cheap Levine way of thinking.' That's why you had to go to work after school when you turned sixteen and got your driver's license, and through your summer breaks and college. It was because Mom was raised cheap. She insisted on it."

Whether this is true or not—and brother Phil says it isn't—I suspect it's part of the old values of Dad's generation where the man was the bread-*winner* and the woman, the bread-*baker*. Yet I was expected to be both, which makes no sense to my questioning mind. How often Dad's answers work for him but not for me! Sometimes I think he doesn't understand them himself, instead putting the full force of his energy behind his decisions on principle—as in my youth with my endless string of "whys?" and his equally tireless response, "Because I said so."

It's clear I'm going to have to figure this one out on my own.

Moshe and I leave the hospital in silence, lost in the labyrinth of our private thoughts. My handsome rabbinical brother leans an elbow on the railing of the stairs, crossing his feet at his ankles while we chat in the parking garage. *If Mom and Dad's not paying for my college education wasn't chauvinism, perhaps it was just confusion,* I thought. *Dad would say one thing and do another. It's just who he is.* Here stand a brother and sister mulling over the incongruities of their interwoven childhoods with the matured minds of adults. I regard my grown sibling with wonderment, grateful that our lives are wreathed into the same tapestry. Moshe adds his impressions about our parents and how they were prepared to do anything to help us materialize our dreams. *Or theirs?* I share my thoughts about Dad's offer a few years ago to put me through medical school. Me, *medical* school? Perhaps he thought the phrase *my-daughter-the-doctor* rolled nicely off the tongue.

"You know, Sis, they insisted that you put yourself through

college simply because you could. They would have covered what you couldn't."

"*Hmm.* Did you know that I got 'sophomore slump' in my second year? I nearly dropped out, especially since I was the one covering expenses. But Mom and Dad talked me out of it."

That's one battle I'm glad to have lost despite my rebellious grumblings. Completing my studies at the University of Michigan in Ann Arbor proved to be an important era in my life, reaching far beyond the scope of academic studies. It helped me to break family ties and take my first baby steps toward discovering what I wanted to do with my life. An industrious string of employment opportunities paid my way through a university education. The jobs scattered across my resume included scale girl in a large grocery store, receptionist at a doctor's office, waitress, campus phone operator, housekeeper for several families, and reader for a blind student named Richard who harbored valiant hopes of becoming a film director. A Bachelor of Arts degree with honors in English, psychology, and a secondary teaching certificate accompanied my graduation.

Moshe checks his cell phone for messages. We conclude our talk about how Mom wanted the boys to pay them back for their schooling but Dad forbade it. This was the biggest issue he claims they ever argued about.

How tactfully the doctors handle the concerns of a man who has just been dealt the harshest blow of his life. Stage-four pancreatic cancer is the diagnosis doled out on the day Dad leaves the hospital. In allowing him the comfort both great and small of returning to his own home to buffer the fateful news, they have shown my father a great kindness. He says something that he will repeat often in the next few months—that it's time for him to move on and for us to be on our own.

"You have a huge appetite, Linnie. Just like your mother." At the restaurant lunch with Jackson and Tommy, he glances up in my direction from behind a wall of newspapers. Often in these last months, Dad will use humor to put us at ease, drawing on his inner sanctum of strength, this time with the recent shocking news of his test results.

"You, Dolly," he says, perhaps in jest, "were more trouble to raise than all your brothers put together." Funny, I'm never quite sure if he is joking. How do you read someone who plays his cards so close to his chest?

"I promise you, Zeke," Dr. Beckwitz says, "the quality of your life won't change." As the months wear on, the doctor's counsel will make less and less sense. Often Dad will feel betrayed by it, shaking his head and repeating as if in a daze, "He said my quality of life wouldn't change."

Perhaps it's truer to say a promise was made that by its very nature cannot be kept. As the disease progresses and Dad's life is considerably altered, I'll tell him over and over, "The quality of your life *hasn't* changed. There's love all around you—though yes, the outer circumstances are changing. Umm, maybe a little." But as so often happens when I speak my truth to my father, my words evaporate before they reach his ears like snowflakes melting in a wintry mist before brushing the ground.

By some mystery that makes life a rich drama filled with deliberately-sewn coincidences, Dad receives his test results on the sixty-year anniversary of his own father's passing.

At his request, I return to his condo just before sundown. Lighting a *yarzheit* candle for my grandfather, thus honoring the traditions of the Torah, means the world to my father. I repeat the Hebrew prayer, "Baruch Atah Adonai." *Blessed art Thou, O Lord, our God.* With open palms I draw in the light of the flickering candle whose flame burns both literal and symbolic. The wax drips with a muffled thud onto a chipped plate on the cracked kitchen counter. I sense that I am alone in a crowd of souls, performing the ceremony for all Jewish children throughout time who have lost their parents and now inhale softly just beyond my vision in the silent twilight shadows.

The next day Dad is released from the hospital just in time to say *Kaddish* for his father at synagogue—one of the most important and central prayers in Jewish liturgy. As these prayers are said only by men, I wait outside in the car passing my time in the stillness of meditation, each breath a droplet of candle wax that evaporates into eternity.

"What a beautiful life I've had," Dad says in repetitive overtones at our after-dinner card game, more to himself than to me. Thus begins my father's closure on his life. Also commencing is his final act of parenting.

He is preparing his children and their children for his departure from this world.

"Now if I lose in cards I can blame it on the cancer." Dad toys with the word *cancer*—its implications, its newness, and how in joking about it he can claim a sense of mastery over his life-threatening opponent that now has a name. His sense of humor has yet to abandon him.

Our hand of gin rummy is interrupted by the telephone. Dad lumbers to the living room and lowers himself onto the black leather couch like a sack of newspapers dropped at a recycling bin. He props his feet on the cluttered Sixties-style coffee table. "Everything will be okay," he assures Robert Katims, his poker buddy. "People get scared hearing the word *cancer*," Dad tells me. "I have to minimize it so they won't be alarmed."

The doorbell rings twice and Jackie Sunshine—or Jackson as we call her to avoid confusing her with my brother Jackie—breezes in like a determined tradewind. People sometimes ask if that's her real surname, which it is. Jackson has just left work. Well dressed and accessorized as usual, she wears the deep colors of autumn leaves ushering each other to their final descent to earth. Her pantsuit offsets her coiffed reddish hair and her freshly manicured nails are fashionably squared at the tips. While Dad will brag unceasingly about his children, he veritably sprouts compliments for this dear-hearted lady who fills his playful spirit to overflowing and accessorizes his days with a passion for life barely concealed by her wide eyes.

They take their seats at the table for an evenly-matched game of Scrabble. Playing all seven letters on her first turn, Jackson enjoys the psychological advantage of an extra fifty points. Even so, Dad beats her. Oh, how he loves the winning! It nourishes and affirms his essence, while seeing them so happy together brings comfort to his family.

"Anytime your dad comes by my place," Jackson tells me, "I can always hear him down the hallway either singing or whistling and, you know, sometimes both." Her Canadian accent like her heady perfume is far from subtle. Dad studies the Scrabble board like a sheepish child being lauded by his teacher in front of his parents. "And just as I open the door, he's finishing the last of his moves. This guy, this Zeke, he improvises some kind of tap dance and soft-shoe shuffle. All for my benefit!"

Jackson leans across the Scrabble board to Jewishly pinch his cheeks in a manner that has caused many children to run from their aged relatives for fear of being permanently scarred by the enthusiastically rendered bruisings.

"Your father, *oy*. He's the king of the *mensches*."

The Backstroke Goddess
of the Waves

"What a good life it's been," Dad says. "*Keinayinhora*, how lucky I am."

"Say, Dad? Do you know where you're going after this life?"

"Yes."

"Where?"

"To be with Mom."

With no prompting on my part, Dad says my mother was crazy about me. "You know, I thought you might be a boy which is why you almost got named Philippa. Your mom, she was thrilled with you. We named you after her Aunt Leah who had just died and my grandmother Rochel, or Rachel; thus Leah Rochel, or Linda Rose. It means *beautiful flower*." Who knows, perhaps my birth name foreshadowed my career as founder of the oldest flower essence company in North America.

To take a new name is common for people who begin a new spiritual path, which is why several decades ago I became Lila Devi. The Sanskrit words mean "goddess of the cosmic drama," *devi* also referring to Light and to the nature spirits or devas, another symbolic connection to my work with flowers. Interestingly, no one in my immediate family ever calls me by this name. It saddened me for many years until the realization came to me, why *should* they? *Linda* is who I've always been to them and always will be. *Linda* as they speak it is heavily accented on the first syllable, landing strongly on *da* as it would be pronounced with a Bronx accent. *Lila Devi* is without accent on any one syllable, perhaps reflecting the even-tempered consciousness of India's underlying divinity hidden beneath its superficial layers of poverty.

Dad continues, ever adept at changing the subject to suit his whims. Smiling but not joking he says, "I'd never seen a newborn before you came into this world, Linnie. You were blue and wrinkled. And the *ugh-liest* baby I'd ever seen." *Ugly* if you ask me, is an ugly word. Somehow my father's exaggeration made it even more so. "Your ma's ma, she gave me such a time when I would talk like that. '*Oy*, Aaron,' she says to me, 'why the *meshugas*?'"

Thus from birth began not the easiest childhood though certainly not the hardest. The moment my father first set eyes on me launched our loving but conflicted father-daughter relationship. Even so, there remains his unexplainable dearness as a channel for my birth. And a love between us that touches our souls far beyond the psychology of difficulty and dysfunction. Dad enacted his role as my father with brilliance and style. The ever-lingering tension between us served as a primary impetus for me to seek a lasting inner peace, one that nothing outward could take from me. This indwelling conflict eventually led me to embark on a spiritual path of my own choosing outside the Jewish faith. *I was to become a yogi.*

Yogic philosophy, as I was to learn, offers an expanded view of a single incarnation in the context of a long chain of many lives. In time I came to understand that my father could only awaken within me certain mental tendencies, or *vrittis*—tiny unsprouted seeds of committed energy asleep in the soil of the energy body, harbored there long before birth. Also I would learn about unconditional love through the yogic concepts of the Heavenly Father and the Divine Mother whose universal truths enliven this chant:

In this world, Mother, no one can love me.
In this world, they do not know how to love me.
Where is there pure, loving love? Where is there truly loving Thee?
There my soul longs to be. . . .[1]

Dad slips into vintage storytelling mode. Seated on his bed while refusing the comfort of the staunch pillow behind his back, he appears commanding, formidable, somehow out of place as he draws anecdotes from the past into the mini-theater of his hospital room. Having just received the news of his condition, the spilling forth of these many oft-repeated yarns seems to bring him peace. Dad begins with his first date with Mom.

You'd think the story had never been told before.

"Harriet was quite heavy back then. Cousin Bernice had outfitted her in a *very* ugly brown dress. I hated that dress," Dad says, bending his square knuckles inward to flex the arthritis from his fingers. The *h* in *hated* became an aspiration, the word *dress* enunciated with a snake-like hiss.

"Still we had a wonderful time."

A fierce blizzard prevented Aaron from using the family car. Midway through the harsh Chicago winter, his hometown streets were laid to rest under six feet of snow. Formless piles of slush outlined the edges of the main roads, and passersby were rendered unrecognizable in their scarves, caps, mittens, and coats as they lopped along the pavement like sock puppets.

"Brother Joe was living in California. My two sisters Betty and Mamie had already moved out, and the rest of us shared the car. But I had to take the bus to meet your mom. First we walked to a crowded restaurant where we had to wait for an empty table. I couldn't help noticing how much water she drank. Here was a gal who knew how to keep herself hydrated! Man-oh-man, was *I* ever impressed. I thought she was trying to fill herself up so she wouldn't eat a lot. Talk about being wrong! Your ma, she proceeded to order—and eat," he added, looking sideways at me with double meaning, "everything on the menu!"

Aaron walked to the cinema arm in arm with his stuffed-to-the-gills date. "The featured movie in black-and-white starred Jane Wyman as a deaf-mute. *Oy,* I was so in love with your mother." The faraway look in Dad's eyes reflects the bright lights of the Midwestern snow.

"So then what happened?" I ask, quietly considering how rare if ever are the occasions when he requires prompting.

"I didn't see her again until the next summer at a beach in Michiana. She'd lost weight and she was *gorgeous*! I'll never forget that two-piece white bathing suit."

"You mean from the old photos?"

Dad doesn't hear me. He's at the lake with Mom. She had excelled as an athlete and was the captain of her high school swim team. Whenever she dove into the water, it welcomed her without a ripple.

"To this day I don't swim well. But Harriet, she swam beautifully. When I first saw her do the backstroke, she looked just like Esther Williams. You know Esther Williams, Linnie? Your ma swam in a way that put that pro to shame. I mean, she made Esther look like a biker."

It was no secret that Zeke was smitten with the swimming pro and truth be told, so were his brothers Frank and Mickey. On a summer's day when the wind and sun vied with each other for attention, playing coyly with the distant waves, the trim Zaret brothers sat in a circle on the shore in their high-waisted swimming trunks, digging their toes into the gritty beach sand. It was left to the fates to decide by the drawing of straws who might win the honor of asking The Goddess of The Waves for a date.

"And I won," Zeke says smiling. How strange to think that one of my uncles might have been my father! "She challenged your Uncle Mickey to a swimming race. Your ma, she let him do the faster stroke, the crawl, while she did the backstroke that's much slower.

That was her way of giving him an obvious advantage." Dad draws in his eyebrows. "Because of the nature of that stroke, the crawl can be accomplished with much greater speed.

"She beat him by a mile. Your mom," he says with a fresh grin, "she was ree-ally something."

My father's narratives are always infused with a sense of Great Lessons To Impart and Something Very Important Being Transmitted that will somehow make us better people for hearing them. But none of us family members are ever quite sure what message he's trying to convey other than simply Dad wanting to tell us stories that we've all heard a million times before. *Perhaps to fill us with the wonder of life. or to awaken our own ability to appreciate its mysteries?*

Or merely for the pure fun of the moment that is a treasure to enjoy before it passes, as he soon will.

For Dad to stockpile these yarns with no audience to hear them—well, that would be unthinkable if not just plain rude. Family and audience to him are one and the same. Little did I know then just how precious these dramas would be once we were left with only the reflections of our memories.

With bravado, passion, and an ability to turn a simple incident through the spoken word into a story worth telling—Dad is teaching us how to live.

January 4, 1949

Dear Beanie Pie,

Just finished talking to you over the phone and, boy oh boy, did you ever sound good. I miss you, your caresses and kisses, your loveliness and beauty and your quick wit. Dolly, I love you. Could go on forever.

The trip back to Chicago was a tough one, both because I had to leave you and because the ride wasn't so pleasant. I'm starting to feel more at home in Detroit than in Chicago. Must be because we are starting out on a new life soon, eh what?

Enjoyed speaking to Mom. Give everyone my best love. By the way, Beanie, you know how young I am and yet you persist in taking advantage of my good nature. I love you, my little sugar plum fairy.

Brother Morr had a little trouble at the sweat baths. He poured some hot water over himself by mistake and so he has a very bad burn. Think I'll see him tonight. It is so cold outside that I hate to even step out of the house for a minute.

Now about work.

We are planning to kill them dead this year. I wrote ten letters today in an effort to learn more about sales techniques. The place was in a terrible condition, as a furnace went on the fritz. What a day was had by all.

I miss you very much. Am going through same stages as before—can't eat or sleep. How do you account for this? Ask yourself why I love you, and then you'll know why, my little beautiful girl. I'll never stop telling you I love you.

Your one and only sprout,

Bean That Is

Until I'm in your arms again, nevermore to roam— I love you!

TENNIS WHITES ON THE
CELESTIAL COURTS

"When I look back on my life, you're the best thing that
ever happened there."

These were Dad's first words to me this morning. *When the
frills and frivolity are stripped away from an incarnation, all that
remains is love.*

The subtle complexities of my relationship with my father in
these next few months will begin to come into sharper focus.
Oh no, there will be no charmed childhood for *this* Jewish princess! I'm not just Aaron's only daughter but the only child of
five whose future he cannot control. As sparring partners we're
evenly matched: in strength, in determination, and—maybe just
a little—in stubbornness. Yet aren't these the very qualities that
will allow me to shoulder the herculean task of live-in caretaker
as his physical suffering and mental anguish begin to intensify?

In his trademark rambling fashion, Dad talks about a lecture
he once gave at a sales meeting. "That speech lasted ten minutes."
He looks directly into my eyes like a teacher holding a wooden

pointer at the blackboard. "When you're selling," he says, "you plant a seed. You make sure you water every aspect of that seed. After my speech, another salesman, he comes up to me and says, 'I want to work for you.'"

Dad *shows* rather than *tells* about his characters, true to the principles of good storytelling—his less-than-subtle way of hinting that he delivered a great speech. His account remains impersonal, allowing any thinly disguised exhibition of self-praise ample margins from a semblance of bragging. As the youngest child coddled to a fault in a large family, he learned to scoop up praise like second helpings at the dinner table. When I laud his rhetoric, my father does not buckle even under the weightiest of compliments.

A rough day. Dad's pain is severe enough to call the doctor. Once he finally admits to needing relief two and a half hours later, we phone the prescription to the pharmacy. Retrieving it takes another hour. The time spent waiting passes interminably slowly and I cannot seem to will it to move any faster.

"I can't believe there's so much pain with this condition." Dad struggles to mask his shallow breaths.

"We'll fix this, Pops, not to worry." I straighten his pillows, feebly conveying a sense of certainty that eludes me. On his journey to Heaven, pillow-fluffing and prayer will give an arsenal of comfort to my father. "I'm so glad you're here, Linnie," Dad says for the first time since my arrival a week ago. "*Oy vey*, how much you're doing for me. I'm so grateful." These tiny, magical moments sprinkle my soul in a garden of memories, especially knowing that so few of them remain.

"Dad, there's something I have to tell you. When the time comes, you won't need to check into a hospice center. *I'll* be your hospice." I dig my fingernails into the lumpy polyester of his pillow, bracing myself to override his opposition.

Much to my surprise, Dad remains silent. Next we establish that he won't be driving any longer. Several serious mishaps behind the wheel on our morning trip to the blood work lab confirm the timeliness of this decision. After making a left-hand turn from the through lane, he then headed straight into the incoming lane, or where traffic would have been had we not been traveling on an empty residential street. This error in judgment left him so badly shaken that for the rest of the day he relinquished the reigns of his autonomy on the road to his daughter. It was the last time my father ever drove. Truer to say, it was the last time we ever *knew* that he drove.

I suspect the latter.

At last. The medicine's biochemical magic casts its spell and Dad beats me badly at our evening game of gin rummy. Thus does he reclaim his lost sense of power.

"I can't thank you enough for being here, Linnie." Dad tenderly assembles the Scrabble game on the pinewood dining table whose attractiveness has long since been scuffed away. "When you and your brothers were kids, I used to come home from a day of sales calls bone-tired exhausted. Your mom would be standing in the doorway in her cotton tennis dress holding her racket. Man oh man, it wasn't even funny. She was ready to head for the courts! So *nu*, we'd play."

"Did playing tennis with Mom ruin your game?"

"It might have but it saved our marriage. We'd play a set. Six-love. Another set. Six-love. And a third, six-two. Then she'd say, 'Now I'm warmed up, Aar. Let's begin.'

"Your mother is waiting for me in Heaven in her tennis whites." My father turns over the minute-hourglass timer with a thump which means I have exactly sixty seconds—no more and no less—to place a word on the Scrabble board or lose my turn. Dad has never played easy with me.

He's not about to start now.

"Linnie, what's with the toilet paper?"

"What do you mean?"

"I mean, why do you have to use so much?"

"*Da-a-ad*—"

"Don't whine," he interjects. "How many times have I told you not to whine?"

"Dad." I correct myself, being less liberal with my syllables and more so with my dignity. "Because I'm a *girl*." Embarrassed and exasperated, my eyes burn hot in their sockets as I stand face-to-face with the only person alive who can make me feel five years old.

"Paper-schmaper, whaddaya talkin' about. Okay then, it's no big deal," he says, skirting an apology.

"You know, Dad, The Depression ended a long time ago. Maybe, just maybe, we don't have to conserve every little scrap of every little thing?"

The next day another rough patch. Not the easiest of days but certainly not the hardest. Or so I think.

The runaway train of errands races nonstop from 8 in the morning until 8 at night. First is our appointment with the pain management specialist. Doctor and patient debate from every angle: should Dad proceed with chemotherapy or will it too greatly compromise his quality of life?

Agonized and unable to rest as the clock strikes midnight, Zeke paces back and forth in his room as though playing the net on the tennis courts. The score is six-love with pain trumping the welcome oblivion of sleep. My father has never in all his life encountered a test he couldn't handle with grace, poise, casual ease. He seems not at all prepared for this cancer-schmancer that strips him to his very soul. Yet even so he will endure, overcome, and—in his own way and on his own terms—survive. What we surmise as discomfort from the pancreatic cancer we're soon to learn is a cancerous liver bruised from the recent biopsy. The meager meds aren't helping. The three-day skin patch hasn't yet hit its stride. To witness my father's pain breaks my heart into more pieces than I can count, rendering me utterly powerless and helpless. These two states of being that he most abhors dig themselves under my skin like tics after a walk in the woods. Inwardly I cling to the living tree of my spiritual teachings to fight my own inner battles and rise "above the storms, above the pain" to "a land where peace and laughter reign."[2]

The digital clock on the nightstand flashes thin red lines in a futuristic font with a robotic mentality, announcing to the world that it's 2 a.m. To distract my father, we retreat to the blessed Scrabble table. Once seated, we wait an eternity for the narcotics to deliver relief to his temple of body and spirit.

But the game morphs into a nightmare.

"Oh, *my*," Dad says softly.

The unmitigated pain and heavy-duty drugs lay wait in ambush. Without any warning, Dad faints and topples over sideways. Why can't I reach around the table fast enough to support him? *Because I'm dreaming and this isn't really happening? Because my father is my hero and always in control of his every move?*

He crashes head-first into the base of the floor lamp. I scoop up his hollow form that lays on the cold linoleum like a broken action figurine. As I watch helpless and powerless, a thin red gash forms above his left eye. I cradle his head on my lap while a series of convulsions runs its course and a swirl of blood and vomit saturate the coarse linen of my nightshirt. Dad awakens disoriented and confused. As if from a deep and peaceful sleep.

As if from a dream.

KERFUFFLE ON THE TREADMILL

Dad shuffles the deck to announce without words that our morning card games are about to begin. He flicks the cards with his squarely shaped fingers, their swiftness conveying that whatever he does, he does well. "Do you think I'm going to take myself seriously after eighty years?" he asks lightly.

"Nu, Dad, when have you *ever* taken yourself seriously?"

Oh no, his corniest joke and I set him up for it. "If you're serious, then I'm Roebuck. *Ba-dum-dum!*" he chuckles. "I don't know how I could do this without you, Sister." Each of his nicknames for his children land on our souls like tiny song birds, expressing different facets of our relationship with him in both familial and familiar ways. When he calls me Sister, I feel his respect as though with impersonal deference he perceives me as a nun. A *Jewish* nun?

Much like a cat in the act of comfort-grooming, Dad shifts into storytelling mode. With bravado and aplomb he entertains his audience, an honor that happens to fall to me this time. "Your mother had such a good experience giving birth to Moshe that she wanted to have another child. Hashem saw that it went beautifully compared to what happened at Harper Hospital." I believe he's describing Jackie's birth. "That doctor gave Mom drugs to delay the delivery just so he could watch the Lions play football.

"And that's what happened. You'll be so happy with your life, Linnie, you won't know what to do with yourself. Take my word for it."

Imagine. Dad's still beating me at cards and Scrabble. But in this morning's game, the taste of victory so sweetly savored, all the more because so rare, is mine.

"You're now equal to Tommy," Dad says, tapping his palms on the table with pleasure and pride that froth into a singular joy. Many times in these months he will brag that I'm now as good at Scrabble as baby brother Tommy. *Indeed, am I finally as good as one of my father's sons?* It occurs to me that maybe all along I've been "one of the boys" to him—not just because I was a tomboy in my youth but because he insisted I hold a job from the day I took my first driver's license for a spin. Brother Moshe had his lawn-mowing clients, I had my after-school jobs. In my father's eyes at last, I've risen to my brothers' status. Through a simple board game, I've finally won his respect.

With the tenderness of a mother, Dad is preparing his loved ones for his departure, wanting us to soldier on when he's gone. While that will be so for each of us to varying degrees, the thought of living in this world without him offers no solace. "So what's not to love?" he asks, more as a statement than a question.

The wisdom of Dad's declining body seems to be redirecting his energy inward. He's sleeping more and doing less. Meanwhile I'm working on managing his overall well-being and fielding a different kind of pain management—more of a pain in the neck. Dealing with my brothers and their uncompromising yet well-intentioned views on how to make our patriarch's life a little easier. We all want to do what's best for him but no one is quite sure what that might be. We've never parented a dying father before and we're floundering. Nor is he willing to let us take control of his life as long as the gift of breath remains within him. As far as Dad's concerned—and whether we like it or not—he's still in charge. What he considers paramount is being able to maintain his mental sharpness. That he can win at his home's equivalent of a gaming table affirms to him that his mind is still fully intact.

Two expressions of his discomfort are causing me concern. The steady pain and the intermittent unpredictable sharp spasms. Dad is tuned in almost psychically to his body, more so with each new shift of energy and emerging symptom. His insights into its inner workings even while losing mastery over them— and an acute sense of how both the medications and the cancer are affecting him—seem to be signs of his deepening awareness. Courage, perseverance, and unexpected humor course freely if not recklessly through his veins.

Indeed, has he ever been more alive?

Being with my father now is a great blessing. For the remainder of my life, I will look back on this time as one of my greatest and most blessed of trials.

The realization dawns on me that despite my best efforts, I've had just about all I can take. Dad is right. *This is too much for me.*

I've lost the ability to endure witnessing what's happening to him. Can I give Aaron the care he needs? This will be one of my many hesitations in the months ahead. The nightstand is filled with drugs, and my mind is filled with doubts. A peaceful meditation follows several slow breaths, each sigh a wordless, formless prayer that allows me to catch my second wind. Once more, I find that I can resume the role of caretaker that encompasses managing endless phone calls, colliding egos, and familial disputes rooted in loving concern.

A difficult evening. Dad cries out for much of the late night and early morning. Like a wounded animal in the wild too distraught to hush his own mutterings, his instinctive survival wisdom is swallowed up in pain. Trying to sleep through my father's stifled gasps and being unable to help him are as unendurable as him saying he's fine and *has* no pain. Is this his coping mechanism to remain one step ahead of the cancer symptoms? To avoid the unpleasant repercussions of the Vicodin? Or to protect his little girl as he's always done from what he perceives as realities too harsh for her to bear?

This cycle of runaway pain I hope will soon be over. *God,*

please let it be so. Dad now has the pain lollipops that we call with mock affection "narcotics on a stick"—the lozenge-type suckers with quicker absorption through the mouth to relieve the sharper, stabbing sensations. My own doctor says there's no reason for Dad to suffer, especially with all the latest advancements in pain medication. He considers the side effects that accompany these heavier medications to be unacceptable options. Thus by his own tenable choice, the mind-numbing lozenges remain in the top drawer of his nightstand, unacknowledged and unopened.

Less than an arm's reach away.

Brother Jackie stops by. He glides dancelike through the narrow hallway lined with the broom closet and the washer-dryer twins. Baggy yoga pants and a loosely fitting shirt poorly disguise my brother's broad shoulders and trim waist. Many are the times his sister teases him, "Hey bro, can I borrow your washboard abs? I'm needing to do a load of laundry."

The heady cellophane-wrapped irises tucked under Jackie's arm when he first arrived now adorn the pine table. The blossoms transform the dining room into a private shrine where endless games have been played while Time Itself takes a time out.

With a glass of juice in one hand and the phone receiver in the other, Dad calls his brother. A fatal heart attack just took the life of Uncle Mickey's son barely fifty years old. The call is clouded in heartbreak. Yet just behind it lies the solace of divine love more brilliant than a thousand suns.

"Mick, I'm so sorry God took your son. I'm sorry He did this to you. A child should *never* go before a parent. I can't think of a reason why this would happen. Maybe God knows better. . . I know, Mickey, I know. . ."

Dad's only remaining sibling, now surviving on dialysis treatments in a Florida retirement community, responds with silence. Jackie holds Dad's hand for the duration of the call like one shallow-rooted redwood tree in a forest bolstering another. The son leans over his father at the dining table, poorly lit by a stand-up lamp on a spring—the very same model Dad once sold to his doctor clients. "I didn't tell Mickey about the cancer. It would be too much for him." The tragic news isn't well-timed for either brother, with Dad suffering from severe pain not yet mitigated by the skin patch that he will rotate on different parts of his abdomen until there is no surface that has not been covered by it.

"I've never seen him so shaken," Jackie tells me while Dad naps in the next room. "It was the hardest speech I've ever heard him give. And with such brotherly love."

An hour passes and Dad sits up in bed. A little too quickly. Before he can down his pills with a glass of juice, another fainting spell overtakes him. This time by the power of a higher grace, I manage to break his fall. I swoop the glass from his hand and set it swiftly on the dresser with the balletic precision of a well-rehearsed bow of the arm, next to brace his shoulders and prop him up on the side of the bed. My father, so small and so vulnerable, appears to be a puppet in my arms whose tangled strings can no longer support his weightless form. I watch the color restore his cheeks as he returns to consciousness.

This loss of control troubles Dad greatly. To his obvious satisfaction, I answer his questions in minute detail, as though reading him the synopsis from one of the musicals we frequented in my childhood just before the curtain rose and the opening song swelled in billowing clouds from the orchestra pit. The surreal nature of the first fainting spell mere weeks ago played itself out like a bad dream. This time we are catapulted to a place of inner silence, a cocoon of grace, an aura of supernal beauty. Dissolved are the defining lines between parent and progeny. With the pure love of family as the conduit for divine love, it seems as though my father has become my child—though he'll never hear this from *his* daughter's lips!

"Hi, Lila." My friend Seva greets me on voicemail. "Thanks for your message. It was so sweet. You answered my silent question about how your dad was doing (voice cracked). Very happy. And I'll keep praying for him. Okay dear one, bye."

And later: "Hi, and thank you so much (voice wavered) for that very sweet message and the update on your father. Yeah, that's amazing, he sounds like an incredible person so full of love for all of you. I'm glad he was able to get back to that place within himself and find his core and just keep going with that. That's really important. Okay sweetie, thanks for letting me know. You take care. You be strong. You know—we're all going to God and that's what your Dad's doing (crying). Bye-bye."

"Dad?" I ask in a relaxed tone during a lazy game of cards. He chews a pretzel stick while I sip an herbal tea. "Is there anything in your life you'd do differently?"

"Not really, Dolly." He places his next card facedown, ginning on me. The bowl I set beside him is brimming with slices of Bartlett pear, green on one side and red on the other, as though the fruit had fallen asleep in the sun one afternoon only to awaken and find itself sunburned and positively smarting.

"Your deal. You won that hand." I shuffle, cut the cards, and hand him the deck. "Dad?"

"What, sweetie?"

"Do you have any regrets?"

"No." He responds without hesitation. "It's been a wonderful life."

When a person dies, it's said that the sense of hearing is the last to go. I suspect that in my father's case, it will probably be his ability to win at games. Little did I know how close to the truth this would be.

The sun sets on the nearby strip malls and apartment buildings, softening into the shadows the poverty of bag ladies shuffling along the sidewalk and the opulence of shoppers loading their treasures into the hatchbacks of their waiting cars. A Fifties movie on the television with Don Knotts, *The Ghost and Mr. Chicken*, polishes off our day. It's light, silly, and predictably dated. Dad lasts for less than an hour of the slapstick script—in his own home, following his own routine, living life exactly as he wishes and precisely as he always has. On his terms.

The telephone jingles. "This is so hard on me, Linda." Jackson struggles with her words like stringing the pearls of a necklace with a dull threader. "I'm trying to stay upbeat, but I'm having a really miserable time."

"Sure, Jackson, that's understandable. Truly. You know, Dad speaks repeatedly about what a blessing you are in his life. How classy and beautiful you are, how well suited you two are for each other, how nicely you get along. When he's around you, he lights up!"

"Your dad. . ." She trails off, leaving her thoughts unfinished and unspoken. The soft jangle of her earrings tinkles through the receiver like astral bells.

Grocery shopping at Ralphs, Dad's store of choice, is today's big adventure. The trip looms larger than usual with his outer life fitting more tightly around him like a favorite shirt that shrunk a full size in the clothes dryer. Not coincidentally, it's the store for which he's clipped the most newspaper coupons. Why so perfectly trimmed into neat little rectangles? Because he cut them with his handy-dandy autoclavable stainless steel suture-removing medical scissors, one of many relics from his career as a surgical supply salesman.

An animated and energized Aaron pushes the shopping cart down the aisle at breakneck speed, his soul driving him in defiance of the disease that is dethroning him from the existence—perfectly trimmed into neat little pieces—that he so loves. There will be more than a few remaining shopping trips in his future. Some with his daughter, some with his sons. Dad savors the joy of each excursion, never quite knowing if it will be his last.

"Whoa, Speedy Gonzales, slow down there!" I cry out to the tune of a cramped calf muscle. Dad arrives at the frozen food section where he will spend what seems like ages matching items with coupons.

"Linda, come here," he commands, scoping out the low-sodium frozen dinner freezer much like the new sheriff in town in a B-movie western surveying his domain. "This coupon saves me fifty cents on pasta primavera. Such a deal I'm getting!

"*Oy*," he says with a heavy sigh, as though the long-suffering nature of the Jewish people sits weightily on his shoulders. "Such a good life."

What luck that the tennis courts are nearby! The welcome relief of exercise helps me to maintain a thin veneer of sanity and a much coveted strength. Two little boys play handball on the cement backboards, oblivious to the impatient person benched nearby waiting for them to finish. They are carefree if not sloppy with the ball. Their giggles-between-hiccups hint that they're joking in Spanish. Somehow I see my father in them. Why, who can say, yet everywhere I look, there he is. My mental database refers everyone back to him. These little ones have their whole lives ahead of them; Dad's life is nearly spent.

A glance at my watch tells me to return home soon, no time to dilly-dally. In truth, it's Dad who doesn't have much time. *We're in this together. Just like he says, we're a team.*

The elastic band on my ponytail loosens its grip, sending a sloppy lock of hair into my eyes. Artfully with one hand, I stuff it back under my baseball cap. The racket that Dad gifted me with—"Here, *take* it, Linnie, this is for you"—is thickly framed and conspicuously outdated. Even so, my sentimental heart treasures it. A few leg stretches, shoulder rotations, and bounces on my tiptoes energize my limbs, much like the tennis legends in the tournaments we watch together on the sports channels. But the perky little warm-up is where any similarity between myself and the pros ends.

The early morning heat settles into the pores of the North Hollywood pavement, followed by a subtle uprising of dry steam that stings my eyes with perspiration and sunscreen. *Ping.* The clean sound of the tennis ball on the racket strings sings in my ears.

Ping. Smashing the ball and not just hitting it is the subtext of my meager workout. *Ping* again. I challenge myself to hit harder and play longer, while my ponytail swishes against my SPF-30-coated shoulders.

Dad's voice echoes in my head, firm and commanding: "Keep your eye on the ball."

Then: "Don't let it bounce twice."

And on my backhand shots, "Turn your racket, Linda, *turn* it."

I feel like my father gripping the grocery cart in a well-lit supermarket aisle, racing against time as it ticks away the precious seconds of each incarnation that we live only once.

Brothers Jackie and Tommy have mastered the courts with a balletic grace. How their sister loves to watch the poetry of their nicely placed shots, and to hear the volley of their edgy Jewish humor rally across the net between plays. When we were growing up, the other brothers probably never even held a tennis racket. Phil was into cars. Moshe was into God.

On the days when I'm not hitting off the backboards, I either traipse on the treadmill or swim in the pool. Other days when Dad needs me and I can't be gone long enough to drive to the gym, I'll walk up and down the condominium stairwell, sidestepping the frayed carpet clumps to check messages on my cell phone by way of keeping my finger on the pulse of my office with its steady stream of enquiries, orders, restocking, inventory.

This aggressive exercise program as my doctor calls it—

doubling my heart rate for thirty minutes a day, give or take—allows me to boast that I have the arteries of a fifteen-year-old. It builds the stamina I need to continue caring for my father. Lately my aggressiveness seems to have turned to ferocity. *Why does it feel like I'm the one fighting for my life?* Truth be told, I'm fighting to live in a higher awareness of death and dying; to find that place within myself free from self-doubt or questioning of my care for Dad; and to help him pass easily from this world and from his loved ones. Can I do it? *Do it, schmu-it, whaddaya talkin' about?*

Meanwhile the sands in the miniature Scrabble hourglass are running thin.

Later in the week on the health club treadmill, *oy*, such a scare I give myself when I absent-mindedly enter my weight into the wrong grid—the one for speed instead of body weight. Two scampering little feet stumble on the belt as it accelerates toward a hundred miles an hour. I try futilely to keep pace with the revved-up equipment. Fumbling for the safety key, I pull the plug only moments before the machine seems about to go airborne. Onlookers on their stationary bicycles glance up from their magazines, newspapers, and mystery novels pretending not to notice the kerfuffle. So this is what a loss of dignity feels like—a rodent on a hamster wheel gone berserk! Were I not so distracted by caring for Dad, I'd probably feel like a complete idiot right about now.

As if his eldest child wasn't kerfuffled enough.

MENTAL ARM-WRESTLING WITH A WORKING GIRL

Indian scripture says from birth the number of breaths in a person's incarnation is pre-determined. Asleep in his bed Aaron breathes, inward and withdrawn as though the act of respiration is already foreign to him. Who knows how many breaths remain like coins in the pocket of the eight-year-old soda pop peddler at the peak of the financial undoing of The Great Depression? Cradled in the downy arms of restfulness with his knees bent and his mouth open, Dad labors. In and out. *Pause*. Out and in.

Soon I will have to learn to live my life within the space of a hollow breath—between his vibrancy and only the memories of his tremendous life force. And to endure the heartache of his absence that will fade in the remembrance of him over the coming years, from tiny heart stabs to faraway smiles.

Indeed, the ethereal presence of God's kindliness permeates this wretched illness. Our patriarch's brief extended time in this world—meaning his passing isn't a sudden one—allows his loved ones to have closure with him. While still strong, he is completing his earthly ties with the family he has birthed, with the attention to detail of one who will not be returning. Recently I coined the word *dynasty* to describe us. I suppose he's taken a fancy to it because he now uses it from time to time. *The Zaret Dynasty.*

"Earlier, I wasn't ready to go," Dad says this evening. "Now I am. I know the pain toward the end will be severe." Our discussion of imminent symptoms as the cancer progresses includes the pain patch on his abdomen that will chloroform even the memory of his discomfort. For the past six days it has successfully dulled the ache of his biopsied liver that is still reeling from the surgery.

A closed fist knocks decisively on a closed front door, announcing Shmuel. Shmuelie as we call him is Zayde's eldest grandson. Moshe pronounces his son's name *Shmu-ell*—in two syllables, accenting the second with biblical accuracy and lyrical prose. Shmuel got his jutting, set chin from his mother's side of the family. From his father's, an inherited ability to project his will with an immutable fixity of purpose. Shmuel wears his two decades well.

"*Nu*, Zayde?" he goads with the challenge of a foreboding undertow along a deserted strip of beach. The two forces of Nature retire to the dining room for a game of gin rummy. Shmuel towers over the table. He rolls back the cuffs of his checkered shirt with the determination of youth, hankering to get on with the business of beating his Zayde. The cards acquiesce to his sleight-of-hand dexterity as though they'd rather shuffle themselves. The deck crackles in the younger man's palms much like dry kindling under a newly lit match. Although Dad just taught him the game, Shmuelie has already proved himself a formidable opponent.

Before his retirement, Aaron gave a fine quality of energy to the medical profession, now returned to him in the form of excellent doctors. All three specialists overseeing his case seem superior, at least as far as I can tell.

Or that was my opinion until Dr. Beckwitz betrayed him brutally, if not unethically. A Tarceva pill incident—ridiculous if you ask me—caused his patient care to take a thoughtless turn for the worse. It's an odd story. Precisely because my father's uncanny sense of luck allowed him to obtain the costly pills through the Veterans Administration Hospital for practically pennies—the first step recommended by the physician's own staff to encourage the agency of their choice to cover the medication expenses— the doctor's treatment slackened to outright negligence. It seems so unfair unless understood in a karmic context where even the worst crimes against humanity can be explained in terms of balancing the scales of action and reaction. This shortcut wasn't what the doctor expected. In fact, it was a presumed impossibility. Is it professional jealousy, or that wherever Dad goes his jovial attitude magnetizes special treatment? Or both?

Zeke has always been lucky. Why? With the artfulness of placing himself in sync with the rhythms of life, luck has no choice but to respond to him. Everyone thought Dad would be denied the pills. Yet much to our surprise, his good fortune magnetized their procurement. The basic principles of energy are as familiar to him as a deck of cards. Luck, he knows, isn't a deaf-mute. Meet it halfway with positive expectations and it will accommodate graciously.

Many times throughout each day, I wring the wisdom from my friend's words as if from a prayer shawl that comforts its wearer: *Dad is going to God.* Again and again as I watch his body fail, I must be a strict taskmaster and remind myself that he's on his way to a better place. On such a journey, this is exactly how one gets there. How one looks. How one behaves. *It's all perfect.* To resist the natural flow of what's happening to Dad will only cause me great mental suffering. I cannot allow my thoughts to wander in that direction. Nor can I afford to court wrong attitudes as his caregiver or his daughter, especially when he continues to set such a good example for his loved ones by comporting himself with such unflagging strength of will.

"Seeing you suffer isn't easy for me, Dad. That's why I'm not keen on you stopping the pain patch to see how you'll do without it."

Our verbal tussle flares into an argument. Sparks fly hotter than a newly lit gas stove burner. Once we settle this issue, others surface in its place. I say he's harsh with me; he says I'm too sensitive. I'm left feeling that we don't really have anything to resolve, or rather there's nothing we *can* resolve.

"I can't thank you enough, Dolly," Dad says in stark contrast to our mental arm-wrestling only moments earlier. "What a *mitzvah* you're getting for taking care of me."

"*Dad.*" My thin voice crackles. "I would do *anything* for you." Circulating enough air through my tightened vocal cords has become a non-issue. My voice drops to inaudible levels before it reaches him across the room like a poorly thrown Frisbee in the sloppy way I toss it with the rim catching on my thumb, causing it to veer a clean ninety degrees off course.

At last Dad relents. The pain patch will remain in place. *Can it be he finally gets that I actually mean what I'm saying?* As we speak, he appears somehow incomplete, hollow, a mere outline of a book not yet written. I notice him trembling slightly. Body weight is slowly dripping from his frame like wax on a lit Sabbath candle. Even as the cancer ravages his body, the flame of his spirit seems to grow bigger and brighter.

"Linnie?"

Dad calls me into the bedroom to initiate our morning ritual. I hand him the newspaper laden with the latest local-to-global triumphs and tragedies that alight like butterflies on villages and continents alike. Once I clean the smudges from his magnifying glass, he checks his stocks. *Doing well today*, his relaxed manner says. He grazes through the sports page, then the weather. Somewhere between 8:30 and 9 a.m. come the awaited calls from the boys on their way to work. I sit on the edge of the bed to ensure that Dad doesn't fall or faint, hand him a water glass for his meds, and watch without watching as he drinks. He completes his toiletries and we sit down to breakfast for a few games at the-table-where-no-one-ages.

"Do I look gaunt?" Dad peers sharply into my eyes, reading me like a polygraph. He fishes around in my psyche for a nonverbal answer, digging beneath the layers of affirmation that I lavish so supportively on him.

"Oh, you might've lost a *little* weight. But your coloring's good." My none-too-convincing answer fools neither of us.

"I know this is a symptom of the pancreatic cancer," Dad says, his square jaw looking even more sharply angled and his thick white hair begging to be combed. "Linda. I've decided to sell your ma's wedding ring."

The morning light filters through the window blinds, directing my gaze to an aged wooden frame where, hanging crooked on the wall as if in rebellion of its own irony is a reproduction of Picasso's *The Lovers*. A sentimental nerve knots in my stomach.

"That ring's a treasure, Dad, and since you asked—well, *sort* of asked—I'm against selling it. Can't we keep it in the family?"

"I want Moshe to have it appraised and sell it so none of you kids will have to pay the high yearly insurance." His vocal tone devoid of any sentiment seems to bounce off the painting. To my father's practical mind, he's simply taking care of details and as always not wanting to burden us. Dad will be Dad forever.

Then he pays me the highest compliment in gratitude for staying with him these past few weeks.

"Sister," he says solemnly as though speaking to a much larger audience, "I'm going to give you all my winnings from tomorrow night's poker game."

"Gosh, Dad. I—I don't know what to say." While silently touched by his gesture, I'm not sure where he's going with this revelation too sacred for words. "But you know you don't have to make a *tzimmes*, right?"

He answers my question Jewishly with another question. "Do you have any idea how much that might be?"

"Not exactly, but it sounds like you want to tell me. *Nu*, go on."

"About six dollars." To someone raised in the poverty of The Great Depression, this *is* a big deal and well worth making a royal *tzimmes* over.

"Wow, *thanks*, Dad. I promise not to spend it all at one time." Offering me his winnings is his way of drawing me into the game, that holy part of his life much like the orthodox prayer minions attended only by menfolk.

"Sure, sweetie." My father dons the deadpan expression he usually reserves for his card buddies on poker night. "Use it in the best of health." This is a saying I grew up hearing from my relatives. It must be either very Jewish or simply something older people— with enough aches and pains stuffed into their years on this earth to value the treasure of good health—say to younger ones.

Dad peruses the newspaper leisurely and absentmindedly while eating little of an already small-portioned breakfast. He sets aside the coupon section like a child at the dinner table who, after finishing his vegetables, anticipates a glorious dessert. "How about a few more bites, Dad?" My subtle encouragement falls on the deaf ears of someone who won't budge when pushed even if he inwardly agrees. "You need to keep up your weight."

"That," he replies softly, "is no longer in my hands."

Good news at the brain CAT scan appointment to check for possible tumors. *Results negative.* Dad tells the receptionist at the diagnostic lab in hushed confidence as though they've been best friends for years, "Colleen, I'm very upset with my girlfriend."

Jackson had sneakily comped the lunch tab before anyone else could grab it off the table including Tommy, Jackie, myself, or Dad.

He reprimanded her sternly on the car ride home. *"I'm* the one who invited you to lunch and I expect to pay. You're a working girl. I never want you to pick up the tab.

"Ever."

CHEMOTHERAPY POKER CHIPS

The mind of a soldier entrenched on a battlefield, weary and worn in ways that the soundest sleep cannot revive, may wander to gentler places—perhaps a scenic spot in Nature with the flutter of birds instead of the din of bombs, or streams of sunlight displacing random bursts of corrosive shrapnel. In time, perhaps the heaviness of the warrior's tests might lighten like a backpack filled with provisions that lessens in weight as he nears his destination. *Maybe*, he thinks, *life will get a little easier as the end of the journey draws near.*

I awaken early with the hope that the last three weeks have been a dream. That my father is well and will live forever. And selfishly, that I will never have to live a single day of my life without him farther than a phone call away.

So I think as I face my hardest life test ever.

The dreamlike reality sinks in as I step more fully into wakefulness. Sometimes upon arising before wrapping myself in the mismatched outfit of the conscious mind, I grab hold of the hem of superconsciousness. These days, I cling to it. In my heart I know that state of pure being will not abandon me.

Last night the din of my worries over Dad's fever caught me unawares. His elevated temperature from the side effects of the chemotherapy—which I interpreted to mean that he might not be able to continue much longer to buy himself more poker chips to stay in this world—as I'm to learn is instead a symptom of his yet-strong body adjusting to the potent medications. The chemo actually will buy him two more "good" months.

The morning sun catches us laughing together at how violently ill this ridiculously expensive cancer pill for one hundred dollars each renders people. Acne, nausea, trunk rash, diarrhea, fever—just reading the list of potential side effects is enough to make one queasy! One contraindication on the pill bottle you'll never see: *Warning. May coax you to the precipice of extinction and then yank you back to the brink of life.* What are they thinking, these people who concoct cauldrons of pharmaceuticals that so torment the very lives they intend to prolong?

"What are they, *mishugenahs?*" Dad asks. His eyes are radiant, shimmering pools of joy. Throughout this ghastly drama, there are places within each of us that remain untouched by the chemotherapy and the cancer. We discuss the busy *Shabbat* and Passover weekend that lies ahead over a breakfast as simple as it is nourishing—if Dad can manage it. Our plans are interrupted by the trill of the telephone like an intrusive errant child.

"Dad, I'm not ready for you to go," Jackie says. "I want you to see the wonderful things I'll be doing with my life."

"I'll see them from Heaven, Sonny."

Later Jackie tells me, "I felt a wave of peace when he said that."

The evening advances and all the activity tires Dad. Winning a hundred-twenty dollars at the poker game mesmerizes him to overbid his energy reserves and he stays out far too late. Despite Tommy's efforts to steer Dad away from the hypnosis of the card table, it's 1 a.m. by the time they finally shuffle home.

The eight-day festival of Passover, commemorating the exodus of the ancient Israelites from slavery in Egypt, is about to begin for the eightieth season of Aaron's life. The fulfillment of his wishes for this holy holiday ranks high on our list of priorities. He instructs me to throw out nearly a hundred dollars of perfectly good food in honor of the Jewish law that prescribes the removal from the home of any pre-Passover items along with all *chametz*, or leavened food.

"This feels good to me, Linda."

"I'm glad. Then it feels good to me too."

The table where Dad fills his pillboxes for the week is decorated with a bouquet of medications.

"I think this disease is a challenge from the Lord. God wants to test my strength and see if I can take the pressure."

The plastic lids click shut under his deft fingers with the same final crispness of his footsteps that even the plushest of carpets cannot dull. Little do I realize how that sound will echo in my memory after his body is no longer around to be sustained by medications—to regulate his blood pressure, control his cholesterol levels, and thin the texture of his blood.

"Sister, this isn't an easy illness. Dying is the hardest thing I've ever done in my life. I'm very lucky to have come as far as I have."

"You can say *that* again." As though delivering a third-person monologue, I hear myself parroting his signature phrase. *Will the act of remembering my father while he's still alive somehow make it easier for me once he's gone? Can I outwit the natural grieving process so it won't catch me unawares in unexpected moments throughout the years to come?*

"I'm trying to figure out why I got this cancer. I'm going to ask the doctor what will happen when my pancreas fails." Dad sings the first few bars of a Louis Armstrong tune, then imitates percussion sounds through his pursed lips. "I want information. I want to know what's happening to me because I intend to stay one step ahead of this illness."

The light spirit of Passover freedom in Tommy's house accompanies the ringing of the doorbell as we join together as a family. Relatives gather from the far reaches of Los Angeles. We seat ourselves in the dining room—brothers Jackie and Phil, Livvie's boyfriend whom we're meeting for the first time, and Tommy's family and in-laws Marge and Myron. Multi-leveled aromas waft across the festive table. Matzoh ball soup swirled with chicken fat. Gefilte fish garnished with horseradish. *Tzimmes* made with carrots, sweet potatoes, and beef brisket clinging furtively to the bone.

Dad eats little. Although somewhat withdrawn, he actively

enjoys the company of his family. The refrain of chewing and laughter abates when the meal is completed. He excuses himself to rest in the back room where the shades are drawn and the feather comforter will tuck snugly under his chin.

"Dad?" I awaken him from his nap. He looks up startled, returning from a faraway place.

"I love you, Dolly," he says with little staccato pauses between his bass-note words. "Now I know why I had a daughter."

In this moment and in these tender words, decades of distance between us fade into already-forgotten memories, replaced by a deep and lasting love.

Later that night, our joy gathers us around the kitchen table to exercise our dynasty's fierce if not legendary competitiveness in a card game called Hearts. I'm the one least-likely-to-shoot-the-moon, which is how a player can quickly gain high points to his advantage. Or so they think. My plan is to throw down my low cards early in the game. *Sneaky? Perhaps.* Yet no one takes Sis seriously. My strategy passes by the brothers who are distracted with joking amongst themselves.

But Dad always knows.

Without saying a word while deliberately looking away, he drops a heart card on Tommy's lead, sabotaging my plans. Looking equally poker-faced, I try not to disclose through my body language that the parent has foiled my efforts. Or so I think.

Dad already knows he has again outwitted his eldest child.

In the mid-morning, neatly tucked between bottle-necked rush hour traffic, the Ananda Center in Santa Monica sponsors my workshop on flower essences for natural pet care, followed by lunch across the street with my host.

"Hi, I'm Garson and I'll be taking care of you today," the waiter announces.

"Hi, Garson, I'm Lila and this is my friend Krishnadas. We're *so* happy to be taken care of by you." Just the way my dad would greet him—friendly, respectful, genuinely interested.

We place our order, chattering away. Krishnadas shares two milestones in his life—about his father dying when he was only fourteen, and later when a severe blow to his head precipitated a life-changing, near-death experience. We share the parallels of our lives, two soldiers "on the front lines" barely able to crawl through our tests—that uncomfortable place where no rest in this world is possible.

"When my wife Mantradevi and I moved to Santa Monica to begin Ananda's Los Angeles center, leaving Ananda Village in Nevada City, I said goodbye to people in a final way."

The ocean's teasing winds entice us to move to indoor seating moments before Garson delivers our veggie burgers.

"May I trouble you for a bottle of ketchup?" I ask.

"Your wish is my condiment." Garson bows theatrically, waving his drink tray in small circles. Waiter-schmaiter. This chap is *far* too overqualified creatively to be waiting tables. He discloses with little prompting that he's a struggling screenwriter, probably like many waiters in Southern California.

Krishnadas dunks his teabag into a mug of hot water and continues his reverie. "It feels like something inside of me is dying, Lila. It's too hard to be in this world with all the suffering. Like seeing the poverty of the Los Angeles street people. I have to keep my *sadhana* very strong or I just flat out can't do this." My friend's years of yoga and meditation have given him an aura of stillness that contrasts sharply with the hustle of the restaurant.

"Right. I know what you mean. I'm going through the same thing with my father."

"Do you mind me asking, is your mom still around?"

"Nope, don't mind at all."

Garson returns. Much like playing his turn in a game of chess, he takes my empty water glass with his ketchup bottle.

"You were saying?" Krishnadas asks.

"Mom passed away seven years ago. You know, as chaotic as my family life was, my folks did okay with my brothers and me. I mean, who *didn't* have a dysfunctional childhood? Talk about chaotic—look at these sprouts on my burger. Don't they look like they're trying to crawl out of the whole wheat roll?"

"I'm sorry. About your mother, not your sprouts."

"It feels like I'm being stripped of what's not real. And left to see what *is* real." I scrunch the sprouts under a wayward lettuce leaf with the same sense of futility I feel in caretaking my father.

"Yes. I know exactly what that's all about."

Two friends. Two burgers. One shared heart.

VOTING ON ELECTION DAY

Time passed quickly for the newlyweds like a train whizzing through a station to its next stop, kicking up clouds of dust and crumpled candy wrappers. With their winter wedding already a swirl of memories in a photo album, Harriet and Aaron ventured out on a sales trip to the Midwest.

The shelves of Chicago's Alba Arts Studio were anything but barren. The business brainchild of Aaron and two of his brothers —with another sibling soon to join the payroll—boasted an inventory of imported gift wares of sleek and unusual trinkets that made the brothers proud. African statues in ebony wood. Clay figurines of monkeys. Planters shaped like buck-toothed rabbits. And miniature ballerinas in perfect angular poses with gossamer skirts of gauze swirling around their knees of kiln-fired clay, standing frozen in their toe shoes as if wanting that moment to last forever.

Dad's brother Frankie, no doubt a reincarnated wizard, had staked his patent claim for the invention of several gadgets reproduced in large quantities. Among them was Alba the Genie. Ask the squat bronzed figure a question, rub his back, turn him upside down, and an answer as if from the depths of an all-knowing source would appear. Not only yes's and no's but whimsical, almost sarcastic responses: "Never mind," or, "What do *you* think?"

Har and Aar nuzzled together in the 1950 Chrysler, driving within the speed limit on a country road in a moment they hoped would last forever. Suddenly a deer catapulted in front of the car. Tires screeched. Aaron swerved the steering wheel, barely avoiding the animal. The downy fuzz on his antlers shone golden in the sunlight.

"I'll never forget that," Aaron said many decades later. "It was so frightening."

Meanwhile another drama was taking place. Having missed her monthly cycle, Harriet suspected a pregnancy, now with symptoms of distress. "*Am I losing this baby?*" she asked.

"Hold tight, Honey, we'll get you to a doctor." Aaron thumbed through the phone book, searching out a specialist in downtown Minneapolis.

"It's a false alarm, Mrs. Zaret." The doctor peered over his bifocals and a stack of patient files. "You're not pregnant, you're having your menses. When you feel a pain on either side of your upper pelvic region, *that's* when you'll be able to conceive."

Time passed and the doctor's words were forgotten. Harriet and Aaron returned to nest in Chicago with his family nearby. Election Day. The newly appointed sales manager of the Alba

Arts Studio at his office desk scrambled to catch the gurgling telephone. "Aar, why don't you come home and vote?" Then with fading undertones, "I'll fix you some lunch."

"Eh, *what*? I'm so busy I can't even *see* over this pile of papers! I'm sorry, Honey. Ya know, I just gotta catch up. I can vote tonight after work."

"No," she said, insistently. "*No*, that's not what I mean. What I'm trying to say is—I'm having those strange pains the doctor mentioned."

Aaron bolted like a deer in the headlights. A set of fingers slammed down the phone receiver. A flurry of bills, invoices, and scribbled to-do lists swirled like candy wrappers on a train platform. He drove home as fast as traffic would allow.

I suppose my father voted on Election Day. Precisely nine months later, I arrived kicking, screaming, and colic-y into this world.

You Are My Sunshine

The second Passover Seder at brother Tommy's once more reverberates with jubilant celebration.

Dad's renewed flourish of energy finds us singing duets to my guitar accompaniment in a light D progression. The songs resound in the airy acoustics of the living room, ambling like livestock in a pasture with no place to go and no schedule to keep. Sugar-plum fairy notes dance in a folksy finger-picking style across the light-gauge strings of my vintage Martin that sits snugly in my arms.

With his sunshine Jackson there, Dad falters briefly on "You Are My Sunshine." Summoning an almost defiant strength as though pitting his will against God's, he breaks into a harmony on the line, "You make me happy when skies are gray." Half-spent and wholly satisfied, he melts into the large armchair, savoring the musical notes like sips of a fine wine whose sacred grapes have danced on Tuscan hillsides. Behind their fluttering lids, his eyes are bright.

The readings in Hebrew and English weave themselves into

the multi-course meal, illuminating the symbology of Passover. Tradition dictates that we sit comfortably and lean to the left in honor of our newly-won freedom from slavery—a custom affirming that the people of the Jewish nation have earned the right to behave any way they please.

We sing again, this time in Hebrew. To our God. How well I remember the lilting songs from my youth! Never will they fade from my child-heart. The men clap their hands and stomp their feet, keeping time with the cadence, while beneath their *yamulkes* their brows furrow in rows resembling the well-trod soil of the Holy Land as they dig deep into the richness of hard-won religious freedom. Meanwhile the children run amuck, having behaved during the lengthy repast as well and as long as they possibly could. The meter of their good behavior, one senses, has just run out of quarters.

Everybody seated at the Seder table hears something different in Zayde's voice. As superb as his bass timbre is, this purer placement of tone and vibrato gives pause to the breath in our own throats. Hebraic melodies cascade from Dad's essence with a fresh depth. They seem to arise from everywhere and nowhere in the room, peeking like impish kids from around hallway corners and armchair cushions.

Aaron draws forth the nectar of Judaic musical folklore. He sings like a cantor, the very one who touched my heart years ago in Hebrew school. Devotion melts and evaporates into each succeeding note. The religion nourishes him with trickles of sweetness that sweeps through his spine. His spirit holds no fatigue, no aging, no disease. A current of Jewish joy infused with orthodox passion surges and recedes in waves that engulf his soul for all in the room to hear. In our Zayde's Passover voice is a blessed confirmation that all is right within him as he claims his freedom in the nation of his inner perfection. Indeed, Zayde is going to Heaven. Even now he is singing with the angels.

And to his God.

My spiritual path of yoga teaches the willing aspirant not to be tossed about by life's waves of transient emotions. True joy, the ancient science affirms, springs not from outer circumstances but from within us. This explains the superconscious bliss that I feel in my deep spine rendering sleep at night impossible, finally to be lulled back into subconscious realms upon awakening in the early morning—those precious hours that hold their breath before exhaling their way into the skittish dawn.

In these trying days, that joy lives within the marrow of my soul.

Dad is sleeping in. I retrieve the newspaper from the foggy doorstep and at 9:35, he stirs and settles into his stories. To one who knows that his remaining mornings are few, each day is an uncharted treasure.

"Boy oh boy, I ree-ally sang last night," Dad says in childlike fashion. He shakes his head in disbelief as though describing someone else.

"You got *that* right," I quote him.

"The voice of Cantor Pinchak I'm remembering seventy years ago at the Russian Synagogue off Douglas Blvd. To get there, I have to pass the shop of the parents of cousin Peter. And about the Cantor." Dad lowers his voice to a whisper so the characters in his story cannot hear him. "We didn't know if it was just a rumor or not but he had food—*food!*—brought in on Yom Kippur to keep his voice strong. No one was supposed to know. *Oy,* such an amazing voice he had. But eating? *On the holiest holiday of the year for atonement through fasting?* Can you imagine! I used to go to that synagogue for the high holidays with my father. *Oy vey,* what a fantastic voice that Cantor had. Sister, did you ever hear of Richard Tucker, the famous post-World War II operatic tenor? He came to hear Cantor Adler sing—the cantor who sang at our wedding. He was good friends with the Cantor, this *mensch* Richard Tucker."

My father commits to immortalizing every detail of his self-created verbal epitaph. "I remember as a kid not making it into the choir." Whether or not this saddens him, he doesn't say.

More memories flood forth from the recesses of times past. By way of closure on his life, Dad is determined to clasp to his heart the treasured keepsake locket of every detail.

"I saw Babe Ruth play baseball. Twelve years old I was, at the game when Joe DiMaggio dropped a fly ball in center field. He got an error for that.

"When I was a young lad in the Navy, me and a couple-a buddies met the actress Rita Hayworth. You remember her, Linnie? Was she ever something! She was staying at a nearby hotel." Zeke as the boldest and youngest of the group was goaded by his bell-bottomed cronies to phone her room. "I got permission to stop by. She'd been drinking and had no makeup on. She was friendly to us all right, but oh *no-o*, I didn't find her attractive at all!"

Light filters through the dust-covered window blinds. I fiddle with my hair clip, not wholly mesmerized by the unfurling of Dad's autobiography as I sit beside his shadow on the bedcovers. His clothes are folded neatly on a chair in the corner. Stillness brushes this perfectly ordinary moment that exudes a divine perfection beyond the illusory nature of time, space, disease.

Before me sits not a dying father but a soul vibrantly alive.

"It's a beautiful life, honey." My father's thinning arms lay outside the bed covers. "Life has been so good to me . . . so good. I won't forget but if I do, you need to tell the boys—" Here he falters, crying. "My four sons, my four sons. Make sure my four sons shovel dirt on my coffin and cover it completely."

Dad sobs. I wrap my arms around him and he squirms, not at all comfortable with this uncommon display of affection from his daughter. Abruptly he stops crying—more I'm sensing to end the melodrama than from reaching the rock-bottom of his reservoir of tears. "We have to be happy right now, not sad." He repeats this phrase several times, perhaps to carve it deeper into his consciousness before changing the subject as he often does by way of maintaining control of the conversation.

"Jackson is so dear to me. I told her not to date other men

until I'm gone. We had fantastic times together. Just unbelievable. When we were in Aruba last year, people would come up to us and say they'd never seen a couple so happy!

"Make the best of your life, Linda." Another tear escapes the corner of his eye. "I'm lucky to have so many kids. I told Moshe how lucky I am. And about Shmuel—his card-playing is just the tip of the iceberg. I see genius in him.

"We have to be happy. We have to show people how happy we are. The Lord is testing me to see how strong I am. I know there's a reason for it."

"They thought I was a millionaire, your Auntie Mamie and cousins Bev and Clarisse when they came to visit us." Dad's wide smile reflects the benefit of a solid ten-hour sleep. "Because I was the first of the siblings to buy a house. Remember, Linnie? That was the first home we purchased. It was on Condon Avenue in Oak Park, Michigan. Everyone in the family had been renters till then. No one felt right about actually *buying* a home. They all looked up to me with great respect and awe. I had two homes to choose from and I picked the more expensive one. *Oy,* and why not? It was listed at nineteen thousand dollars."

How Dad loves to brag, being only slightly more humble when the subject is himself. That he is his own best audience has a certain charm, as in his account of Mom's final round in the hospital where she spent her last days.

"A male attendant said whenever Moshe came to visit your

ma, all the nurses and staff would straighten up and stand at attention. The man wanted to know, 'Who is this person?' since he was obviously someone very important. So the hospital being Catholic, I explain, 'My son's a rabbi.' To help the guy—a Gentile—put things in context," Dad says under his breath as if stifling a sneeze, "I tell him, 'Jesus was also a rabbi.' *Nu,* so he asks me, 'What's your son's status in Judaism?' and I say, 'He's the equivalent of a *car*dinal.' Once the guy learns this, he too would stand at attention whenever Moshe came to visit."

No one loves Dad's stories more than Dad himself.

"Thank you for coming, Perfecto, but we won't be needing your help," says the-King-of-the-North-Hollywood Castle.

Quick to assess people and form opinions whether they're accurate or not, Dad intuits that Perfecto isn't the right personality match for him. The Filipino health care assistant so newly arrived for an interview is, within minutes, politely dismissed.

As unwilling as Dad is to receive the ministrations of others, his commentaries are never-ending. He saves some of his best for the people who come to care for him. Leaving is not an option until Perfecto hears one of Dad's finest accounts—how at nineteen years of age he ran a sixty-six bed psycho ward in the naval hospital. Ah, but my parent is just getting warmed up! I feel a little sorry for the hapless, soft-spoken man whose comfort is of no concern to my father. Perfecto shifts his legs on the couch to tie the laces of his immaculately white tennis shoes that don't need re-tying. Clearly Dad is enjoying his audience, even though it's patently obvious the favor isn't returned.

"And that's what happened." Dad's voice limps to a halt like a broken windup doll as the ruffled man moves slowly toward the door.

Shortly after 10 p.m., my father reclaims his strength by beating me in gin rummy. *Is this all a show so I can leave for home and not worry about him?*

My prayer to God is for my father's transition to be a joyful one, for him and everyone around him. When I hear his resonant "Dad" voice reverberating off the bathroom tiles, tapping into his musical repertoire from Frank Sinatra to "She'll Be Coming 'Round the Mountain," I know that prayer is being answered. Dad serenades me with "You Are My Sunshine." The song filters into the kitchen while I busy myself preparing his breakfast of prepackaged oatmeal. Everything must be cooked in the microwave, at his insistence and with no exceptions, least of all the morning gruel.

Not one to ask for help, the family patriarch never hesitates to give orders.

"Use the white bowl, Linnie, not the brown one." Dad doles out meticulous instructions. "Follow the directions, Dolly, and then add another tablespoon of water so it doesn't dry out." And again, "Set the microwave at thirty seconds. Then you can rotate the oatmeal and add another ten seconds. Thata girl."

A baseball game blares on the television. Dad sits on the couch and fidgets with his breakfast by way of masking his growing disinterest in food, pretending it might be harboring bugs. Again he brags about Moshe. "Mom had your brother tested, and we learned that he was in the highest one percentile in intelligence. Worldwide."

Dad takes a bite of the perfectly-nuked oatmeal. "So the rabbis, they snatched him up."

Bombs and Battles in the Yeast of The Psyche

Whenever people talked about Zeke—the name bestowed on him by his Navy cronies—the first feature they noted was his smile. Laughing lips and even teeth framed the smile of someone who treated a battlefield as a mere dance floor. The handsome young man stood proud in his naval uniform of bell-bottomed trousers and a matching waist-length shirt. Wearing his white sailor's cap cocked to one side, he greeted life with a sense of whimsy much like a character actor in films of the Forties.

World War II raged overseas. Like most young American men, Zeke felt called to enlist. The United States Navy fueled his patriotic passion with a hunger for adventure and a chance to serve his country. The sailor was assigned a job on base at the eye clinic examining potential officers. Zeke performed his duties with the precociousness of one who had graduated a year early from high school. With the grace of a dancer, he scheduled appointments for eye exams and surgeries and administered the test for colorblindness using the charts with small dots and numbers.

An announcement on the bulletin board one day caught the sailor's eye. Volunteers were entreated to enroll in the first of twenty atomic bomb tests on the Bikini Atoll Islands in the South Pacific. The first explosion had taken place in New Mexico; the second in Hiroshima; the third in Nagasaki.

Life in all kingdoms—animal, mineral, plant—was utterly decimated. In all its destructive glory, The Age of Atomic Energy had begun.

'Sign up for this exciting way to serve your country!' the leaflet entreated.

"So my pal Vern signs up and I sign up," Zeke said, "and *he's* accepted and I'm *not!*"

The young sailor reported to his commanding officer. The stout man's uniform in the days before spandex stretched tightly across his chest. His eyes were all but lost below twin jungles of wiry eyebrow hairs that perched on his forehead like tangled undergrowth in a tropical rainforest.

"I didn't okay you to go," the officer stated with resignation. "I've only got four months left to my term of duty. I have no intention of retraining anybody for your job because you do it so well, sailor."

"Sir, if I may speak? I enlisted in the service when I was seventeen. The war ended in Germany and then it ended in Japan. And I haven't even been aboard ship!" Zeke sighed heavily with a passionless smile. "What am I going to tell my kids? That I was in the service and didn't *do* anything? With your permission, Sir, I would ree-ally like to go on this mission."

The officer bristled with impatience. He lumbered to the

window, projecting his thoughts toward the grounds outside. *Who does this young scamp think he is anyway? Why, he's as green under the collar as a wheat field in pollen season!*

"I'm sorry," the officer said unapologetically while staring absent-mindedly in a self-absorbed reverie. "But this is what I've decided. It's best to forget about it."

A closing glance at the dapper recruit wordlessly excused him from the room.

Some years later, Zeke met a doctor who had been accepted for the Bikini Atoll nuclear test mission. The man had been rendered sterile. Ten years after the first explosion, it was discovered that none of the volunteers were able to father children. Some of the men previously had children, proof of their former fertility. Studies were conducted for conclusive verification and information was compiled. The men who populated that pilot test mission— as many as 10,000 including Vern—had been subjected to radiation without protection.

Vern eventually married. He became a doctor and adopted three children.

"So that's how I was able to have five children." My father chews the plastic mouthpiece of his unlit pipe.

And I'm glad to be one of them.

Engaging the full strength of his soul, Dad fights me on two issues. Home care and driving. Our verbal sparring is evenly matched, with his will pitted against my own. Need one question that the final score ends in a tie? Even though I'm still shaking and ready for a good cry several hours later, I manage the temerity to center myself and hold true to what I believe to be right. Indeed, I've fought my father as he would want me to fight—with courage, conviction, and *chutzpah*.

Dr. Beckwitz breaks the tie at our appointment the following day. *"No driving, Zeke.* You know it's not your low blood pressure that's causing these symptoms, it's the chemo. And the cancer."

"That *meshugenah* doctor," Dad tells me after the office visit, "he doesn't know what he's talking about. What is he, *nuts?"*

A great sage once said that our spirituality is tested in the cold light of day. Such indeed is my test. Many times I remind myself what's important—not the events that are happening but how I choose to respond to them. As if our verbal tussles weren't enough, my parent's behavior has wrung me inside out with his harshness and monumental stubbornness. Tears rise through the layers of my psyche like bubbling yeast in a bowl of warmed bread dough. Oddly, they are helping me to work through these knots of tension.

Dusk settles in layers on the freeways and oceansides of Southern California as our family gathers at Moshe's house for a mid-Passover meal. Aaron's four sons arrive. One by one they enter as if on cue through the arched front door, their work schedules and city traffic permitting. The waning daylight trickles through the stained glass window in the stairwell, while the siblings converge from a radius of many miles across the sprawling City of Angels. My Guru called Los Angeles "the Benares of the West," considered to be the holiest city of India. For all its outer chaos of character, Los Angeles cradles a deep hunger for truth within its half-dormant spiritual slumber.

Dad received his second chemo treatment earlier today. It has tired him greatly. Even so, he eats well and we remain at Moshe's a full two hours, allowing Dad to meet his youngest great-grandchild Chaim for the first time. Softly in awe of new life, he crouches beside the stroller. He extends his hand to the newborn whose disproportionately large cheeks make him intolerably cute. Chaim wraps his pudgy hand around my father's thick-knuckled index finger. Zayde's eyes reflect the miracle of his ever-expanding family—his legacy, his immortality.

Home again. Dad retires early before calling out to me. The morning's argument has left my spirit raw, and I feel I cannot absorb any more. The romance of hearing legends from his youth possibly for the last time has faded. Sorry though I am for the admission, I'm eager to leave Los Angeles for the comfort of my own home. Caring for my father is a cold-light-of-day test, and one that leaves me grateful but smarting sharply. Our talks, to my mind, are often cloaked in futility with Dad seeming oblivious to his own behavior. Some weeks ago when I approached him with a hopeful outcome, no response was forthcoming. Why try to work toward some kind of resolution when these patterns of being seem so psychologically calcified?

The pre-chemo IV laced with anti-nausea medication and steroids is noticeably affecting my father's personality. Of this, I have no doubt.

Dr. Beckwitz assures me there's no documented proof to substantiate the changes I'm seeing in my remaining parent.

A Hymn-like Hotline to Divinity

At last. A brief visit home to the Sierra Nevada foothills allows me to attend to business before returning as quickly as possible to Southern California. Do the deer, squirrels, and foxes feel the joy that seems to rise like geyser steam from the soil and soul of this spiritual community?

"Linnie, *guess what?*" Dad tells me over the phone. "Me and Jackson played Scrabble last night. What a fine player she is! Just fine. I lost to her by only six points." How he loves the thrill of those close scores. No matter what the final numbers are, Dad always plays against himself. A driven man, never will he compromise his standards or settle for mediocrity in any of life's games. "We ordered in a pizza. I didn't like it, Linda. It didn't agree with me. My tastes are changing and I'm seeing things shift in my body." His words slur together in a string of unbroken syllables despite his struggle to wrestle them apart.

"That's understandable." I grapple with my own speech, hearing it stumble lamely through the telephone mouthpiece. *Tell me,*

God, what can I say to comfort my father? How can I show rather than tell him that everything will be more than "just fine?"

"*Nu*, I'm doing everything I'm supposed to do." He begins to cry. "I have to go now, I'm tired."

"That's okay, Dad, we can talk another time."

"Love you, Baby."

The phone line slices into a crackling silence. My father has no tolerance for the powerlessness of tears, least of all his own.

Ever with me is the support of my friends. Sharon, a retired hospice and home care nurse, somehow always manages to say the right thing at the right time. Take for example, our phone talk about the difficulty of convincing Dad that he shouldn't be driving. "There are times, Lila, when you have to do things in a family that aren't pleasant for the person and it's important to have him there for the discussion. You need to decide on your position: 'Dad, this is how we feel about it and these are your choices. Living alone isn't one of them.' This hanging-on behavior is normal for people who want desperately to hold fast to their independence. Giving up driving is a huge part of the picture for them. You'll have to take the keys or your dad *will* drive. He knows how to work this to his advantage. Independence is what every human being wants, and that's what driving represents to your father.

"Mostly, elderly people don't want to burden their kids. You and your brothers have to agree, and you must all be there when you talk to him. Give him a choice so he still feels he's in control because that's what he wants. *Lila, this situation is so hard.* The very best thing is to get the doctor's support. When you break the news to your father, it would be ideal to have the doctor's backing: 'It's no longer safe for you to be alone.'

"Sometimes you can't save people from themselves. My husband's mother fell again and again, even though we tried in many ways to intervene and stop these accidents."

The brothers and I have several phone conferences. This man—beloved of us all and for whom we'd do anything—has united us in a tribal bond. How exactly do we parent a father who will do anything within his power to defy us by way of maintaining his independence?

"Dad needs more protection," says doctor-brother Phil. "I don't think he's safe. Something needs to be done, and it shouldn't be left up to him." He adds somberly, "Dad will be resentful."

"At what point do we no longer honor his decisions?" Tommy asks.

"Guys, Dad might have us hypnotized into thinking he's doing better than he actually is," Jackie says.

"His lifestyle choice isn't the proper one," Phil volunteers. "Dad adamantly wants to continue living alone. He told me himself he can manage just fine."

"Just fine—with the possibility of *fainting*?" Sis asks. "And with *driving*?"

"Let's get him some live-in care." Moshe's rabbinical wisdom enlivens the conversation. I imagine him touching the cords of his *tzitzit* to draw on the inner reinforcement of Judaic law.

"Dad dismissed me today," Phil says, "but I think we should intervene."

Sometimes you can't save people from themselves.

Another conference call rallies us kids into a discussion of the many awkward issues in caring for Dad, who plainly doesn't want our help. It becomes the verbal equivalent of a football huddle—though nobody's quite sure who's the quarterback calling the next play. *Why do I feel so driven to transcribe every possible detail of our communications? Will this somehow make the loss of Dad a little easier, a loss that day by day marches closer to us all?*

We dissect a variety of topics:

1. Everyone wants to hear about Moshe's visit today with Dad.
2. Home care with health aide Victor is recommended by Tommy's wife Liz who expressed her concern about Dad. Starting when? ASAP. Moshe will take care of it.
3. Not having Dad put up the money. Tommy says he'll front it and we can all cover it.
4. Medications. Already a lot in place. Tarceva?
5. Dr. Beckwitz said a home health care aide will provide a hospital bed, commode, wheel chair, shower seat, shower rails, and walker. A Medicare option is also possible. While

still giving palliative care, they say the hope remains to extend length and quality of life. Hospice will step in once the chemo finishes. Victor should start right away.

6. Tommy talked with Beckwitz today, a good talk. Tarceva gives a twenty-percent chance of living a year, only five percent with IV alone. Downside? Expensive. Get it through a Canadian pharmacy.

7. Holter monitor okay. Cardio okay.

Our conference call summarized:

1. Tommy will talk to Dad: Tarceva is covered financially, try it for two weeks.

2. Phil and Tommy will cover the expenses; all concur this should be fronted from Dad's estate without his knowing.

3. Moshe will speak to Dad to confirm that Victor is scheduled for tomorrow.

4. We all agree on immediate home care with Victor coming in for several hours daily.

5. Linda says she'll schedule several Los Angeles visits, going home only to get her business in order.

6. Phil says Home Health (covered by Medicare) will step in and furnish equipment.

7. Moshe will supply a third car when Linda visits.

8. Jackie, who is on the car lease with Dad, will take over the lease and transfer the legality. About insurance: Jackie needs to talk to Ford Motor credit.

9. Appreciation is given to Linda for Dad's care.

10. Moshe: expresses admiration for us all, saying this is a

tumultuous time and we should never lose sight of the opportunity to grow closer as a family. "Let's not take our eye off the ball for unity."

11. Jackie suggests a weekly conference call for Dad to talk to all of us at once, not for business but for a family gathering. We'll talk with him next Monday at 8p.m. Call same number, same access code unless Leeby emails us otherwise.

12. We football huddlers decide to make our closing statements in order of our age, the same as posing for family photos:

Linda says she hears so much love in all of you for Dad and for each other and paraphrases Dad's words that she's very proud of all of you.

Phil says he's going to break out in tears but we're going to get through this, and we'll do the best for our father.

Jackie says what's amazing is this phone call feels like we're having How Kow Chinese food together. This is what Dad wants and Jackie feels it.

Moshe says he already spoke.

Tommy comments as the baby of the bunch and the family rug rat that he has a different perspective, that he loves each and every one of us and wants to thank us for giving of ourselves to him. He likes that we're coming together at this special time.

Great teamwork, fine sportsmanship. Go, guys!

God moves in a mysterious way, prophesied the English poet William Cowper. The hymn-like words of centuries past flow through the telephone line in my friend's lyrical counsel, coming to the aid of a woman-child struggling with the imminent passing of her father.

"Sharon, about the chemo? I'm questioning its benefits for Dad."

"The bigger picture is that we can tamper all we want," she says, "but when it's time to go, it's time to go. When it's your father's time, he'll pass. You may be ready. Or not. I've watched families endure long horrible endings. Especially with pancreatic cancer things can block up and then the end comes really quickly. One day a person is walking around and the next day, dying. It's an unusual cancer. *When the time comes, Lila, you'll be able to deal with it and you'll have the needed resources.*

"As long as your father can call the shots, he should continue to do so. I've had patients refuse a hospital bed until the very end. You really have to honor his wishes.

"This is especially true of men. I once worked with a thirty-four-year-old man who didn't request a hospital bed until the day before he died. Women are more accepting while men are more macho. They'll say things like, 'I'm capable and strong.'

"When a person is bedridden *and* he stops eating, moving, and drinking, he could be close to passing—though there's always the exception. Look for these signs. When that time comes, he'll be more in the other world than this one. He may transition into Cheyne-Stokes breathing—a pattern of drawing in a few breaths, pausing, taking a large inhalation, and then beginning to breathe anew. This may continue for a few days and it often means the end is near. Human will power plays such a huge part."

"Just before my mother passed," I add, "we had to leave her bedside so she could feel free to leave this world. One of the nurses told me, 'Your mother must be either very loved or very rich.'"

I breathe in the poetry of my friend's words. "Families want to be at the bedside. Yet it's often when they leave that the person passes. We all want death to happen a certain way, though it rarely goes the way we think it will." Sharon reads my soul like a dollar-store novel. Little did I know then how true her words would prove to be.

About Dad's poker game winnings of four hundred dollars, she adds, "We don't ever really know what's going on or what someone's timing is. My mom was in a nursing home for nine years. I prayed to God, *what good does it do for her to hang around?* Someone told me that my mother brought joy to the nurses. Who knows? Maybe that's exactly what your father is doing with his poker friends.

"Our prayers have their own intelligence and they manifest as God wants them to.

"Just because your dad is on narcotics doesn't necessarily mean he's doped up. Often the adjustment period of grogginess passes and the body adapts to the medication.

"Listen to your inner guidance and your own wisdom will follow. The main thing, Lila, is to tune in to what your dad wants. Encourage him if he refuses to use a walker when he may need it. You can't make him do anything he doesn't want to do. I've seen people resist strongly until they finally get scared enough. Then they're more accepting. People resist because they see these support tools as a sign of weakness and degeneration.

"Usually there's a poor appetite and then further decline sets in. When the chemotherapy is over, you'll want to contact hospice. You get nurses, aides, and social workers who can help with the emotional issues. They're a great support system. Maybe for your father it can be both—hospice *and* Victor. Sometimes it's better to be the daughter and not the caregiver, Lila, and let the staff fight the battle. That will give you the kind of quality time you both need right now. A lot of healing happens around a deathbed. It brings people closer, and buried issues surface. Families unite if there's harmony, and with the energy you can bring from a centered place, you can be that calming force. You might say to your father, 'Is there anything you'd like to say to Noah, any advice for when he's growing up? I'd be happy to write it down for you.' Personally, I like the idea for a revered and respected grandfather to write a letter to each of his grandchildren. Writing can be a good way to help him process for himself, and you could encourage it. In fact, you could create a photo album for the children to get your father reviewing his life.

"Give him time. He'll come around."

Well, I did and he didn't. It's simply not Dad's style.

My friend quotes the Divine Mother, the feminine aspect of God as revealed to Paramhansa Yogananda, words that span the wisdom of all true religions: "What more dost thou need than that thou hast Me? Dance of death and dance of life—know that these come from Me. My child, rejoice!" [3]

Sharon's last drop of advice is to stay centered. "Remember, just relax and enjoy this time. All of it! Even your father's rudeness. We need to make our energy bigger than what happens to us—to rise above it and not be consumed by it."

In a dreamlike state, I hear what I need to know through Sharon rather than from her, and also what I'm not quite ready to hear. She is my hotline to divinity. "Lila, you'll do this well."

God moves in a mysterious way,
His wonders to perform.
He plants His footsteps in the sea,
And rides upon the storm.

My Dearest Brothers,

Favorite Sis here. How are you guys?

Some of you have called to let me know how well Dad's doing, and that's wonderful. I'm coming back anyway. (Moshe, this Tuesday, Burbank Airport, Southwest Airlines, flight 1090, arriving at 4 p.m. Thank you for your kindness in picking me up. I'm remembering that Dad has IV therapy at a quarter past one, so he and Victor should be home by the time we get there.)

Just so you know, I'm returning now precisely because Dad is doing so well—to have quality time with him and also to give him support in whatever ways he wants. He still has more stories to tell that I'll transcribe for all of you (as if you haven't heard them a million times before!), more songs to sing, and more games to play. Dad told me—again—not to come. But I know he'll appreciate a visit. I can be the twenty-four/seven care that he doesn't want to ask of anyone else. So I'm looking forward to this next visit and to seeing all of you. Very much.

These times with Dad are more precious than ever . . .

Question: shall we still have our Monday 8 p.m. conference call with Dad? I'm game. Moshe informs us that we can call the same number and extension as before. Moshe, can you send this information to everybody?

Guys, do you agree that our family is bonding more deeply? This is very important to Dad. He expressed this wish to me months ago even before the cancer symptoms began: "When I'm gone, I want all of you to stay close." What a gift we're giving him that he can see this happening while he's still with us!

Brothers, you are all so dear. See you soon.

With deepest love,

Favorite Sis

Oh, and P.S. I love how each of you calls me Favorite Sister. It beats being called your Only Sister, a lesser title I might have gotten by default.

One more p.s.: Sorry this isn't a longer letter! Ha ha, just kidding. Given half a chance, I can be very funny—you know, without that dry-with-a-twist-of-Jewish-sarcasm edge that you all seem to love. Though Jackie said recently, "Sis, you have to know when you run anything by your brothers, you're playing to a stadium." I do love you all. And that's no joke.

Families grow closer if there's harmony and with the energy you can bring from a centered place within yourself, you can be that calming force.

Dear Guys,

Once again, I thought you'd like these notes from our conference call before talking to Dad today:

Phil:

He sees the Tarceva making Dad more energetic. It works by trying to suppress the tumor growth. Both the Tarceva and the IV kill rapidly dividing cells. Faster-dividing cells are not allowed to propagate. Dad appears happier and his overall state is good. The meds may tack on a couple months to his life. Phil sees an immediate effect.

Beckwitz may choose to do scans in two months. Phil doesn't know the doctor's plans. He says this is an unpredictable illness.

Jackie:

Were you able to get the walker and the hospital bed? Myron got him a great walker. Phil says Dad doesn't want it, he doesn't want anything that makes him feel like an invalid.

Dad's car: Jackie will do as much of the lease/Ford Motor as he can to switch insurance and get information.

Moshe:

Dad expects there will be a fifty percent tax on the stocks. Is there a way to avoid it? He says we could each walk away with some significant stocks with no depreciation. Somebody has to find out with Michael or the accountant. Tommy will email his accountant.

Very sad for Uncle Mickey to hear about Dad.

Moshe has a white mini-van. Can Linda drive it? Hearing it described, she thinks not, it sounds like a clunker.

Tommy:

Phil arranged for Tarceva, talked about Canadian company with quality control. Tommy got fourteen pills from the discount pharmacy. It's having a very good effect on Dad and he's put on three pounds. Tommy says he's happy to see Dad laugh.

His question is, what to do when Dad runs out of the supply of Tarceva? Dr. B. wants Dad to be rejected by the VA Hospital in order to be accepted by the other agency. Phil offered to take Dad last Saturday, but Dad wanted to wait till this week. If the VA doctor refuses to refer him or if a snag happens, the pharmaceutical company might step in. What to do in the interim? A Canadian doctor talking to Dr. B. may have pills Fed-exed.

Linda or Victor will take Dad to the VA Hospital this week.

We all agree: Dad should have the continuity of Victor's care for part of the week and that having Victor's help should be Dad's call.

"I love you, my wonderful kids, I love you." Dad sings unmelodically, joining us on the conference call. "You are the apple of my eye—except I really like oranges."

"You sound like Rudy Vallee," Phil says.

"I was trying to take an early nap." Dad's mock-Yiddish accent restores the levity we are all struggling to excavate from within the caverns of our hollow hearts. "And now all five of you wake me up."

"Good one!" Tommy says. "Great use of group guilt, Pops. Way to go."

"What's the score of the basketball game?"

"*Nu*, Dad," says Moshe, "how was your day?"

"*Oy*, it was very nice. I got lots of phone calls. The last call said my time was up on the car I gave to Jackie."

"Good. Very good," says Phil.

"I'm glad you guys are sticking together," says Dad, "and you should continue to do that. Everyone's happy? Let's have a hip-hip-hooray for your old Dad. Okay, that's it for now and be well."

"What's with the shortage of songs?" Tommy asks. "How about one more, 'Dai-Dai-Aynu?'" Dad sings a verse.

We all say goodnight, as I say now to all my precious brothers.

Love,

Favorite Sis

A lot of healing happens around a deathbed. It brings people closer.

A Bum Like Me

October 7, 1949

My Dearest:

Three letters from Baby today. Wow! Do you know that you almost didn't receive a letter from me tonight? I became so involved in that book Citizen Har Levine. It is a marvelous book. Thank you, my dearest. How did a bum like me get so marvelous a person like you? Can't understand it. Baby, I'm very tired tonight so you will have to forgive the scribbling. Please?

Mom loved your letter today.

Nice day at the office. I worked very hard for a change.

Five packages railway express.

Five packages truck line.

Four packages parcel post.

(That's nine hundred dollars.)

We had Al Flax check our books today, it seems we had an excellent business the past year. All the boys were honest, and so things checked out perfectly. We learned that practically all of our money was made from October tenth to January of last year. This year we anticipate twice the volume. Work! Work! Work!

Morrie didn't sell a thing today. Selling is very strange. Yesterday it didn't stop raining; today it was a beautiful day.

Back to C.H.L. What a thrilling life I lead. Love letters and C.H.L.

Loving you brings me all the excitement and enjoyment I need.

Your baby,

Aaron

P.S. Love to all the folks. Love ya.

THE HUGS IN MY BACK POCKET

A flea hitchhiked a ride on my body from the Sierra foothills to the Los Angeles coast, managing to wriggle himself into the folds of my clothing and leave a blazing trail of half a dozen angry bites across the real estate of my skin. Discriminating of palate, he chose the softer, meatier, more-prone-to-itching places. Several tender spots remain much to my displeasure, bearing testimony to the insect's creative geographics and survival skills.

Time spent in the presence of a loved one in the dying process can be an altered blissful state. It compels me toward immediacy with an urgency to stockpile in my heart each tiny vignette of preciousness with Dad. Every moment feels so resilient yet so fragile. My internal homework is to reach a deeper understanding of the dying process, of physical death, of the undying joy of the soul—and to survive this blistering test.

Listen to your inner guidance and your own wisdom will follow.

Dad is in great spirits when I return, though the physical decline continues. His songs, jokes, and expressed gratitude for his wonderful life barely mask his fear of leaving this world and his desire to remain here to see his children grow.

Much transpires each day. Spending last night at Tommy's meant that Dad could play four hours of cards with his poker pal Mortesa. To no one's surprise, Dad was the big winner of the evening.

"Do you have a kiss for me?" I ask Noah when we first arrive. We settle ourselves on the living room couch while throughout the neighborhood the ocean whispers its nearness to the stately homes of Pacific Palisades.

"No, but I have a hug in my back pocket. *And* a high-five."

"Can I have the hug and the high-five?" He gives them both, freely and carefully. Zayde naps in the guest room while I unpack upstairs. "So Noah, why did you decide to let Auntie Linda stay in your room?"

"'Cause—because I love you."

The fortress of the five-year-old's room houses toy trains, model trucks and cars, and a colorful assortment of stuffed animals. A child's sanctum, it holds the wonders of youth. Noah creeps stealthily in unannounced and without knocking, sidestepping the morning shadows. His eyes widen to find Auntie Linda sitting upright in his bed, wearing her leopard jammies and meditating to attune to the wonders of the-soul-that-knows-no-age. Authoritatively with his hands on his hips like the CEO of a large corporation, Noah insists as though responding to an unasked question, "I'm in my pajamas and I *need* to come *in* and get *dressed.*" He towers before the dresser and rummages through its drawers.

"Hey, buddy, do you have a hug for me?" I ask.

THE HUGS IN MY BACK POCKET

A wave of seriousness furrows his boyish brow. "I'm sorry to say I ran out of hugs last night." Noah shakes his head of brown curls and raises his narrow shoulders with a likeness to the young Aaron selling sodas in the slums of Chicago.

"I've got twelve hugs in my back pocket, plus sixteen high-fives," I confess. "Would you like them?"

"No. Give them to Zayde."

"And if you had one wish, Noah, what would it be?"

"I'd wish for a million wishes. Seriously, Auntie Linda? Actually, I'd wish Zayde would live forever. You know, it's too bad I never got to meet Bubbi."

Every moment: resilient yet fragile.

The saga of chemo and cancer hums its tune—the sorry ballad in which our family now lives.

A troubling pain on Dad's head overwhelms him once we return home from Tommy's. Unsightly red blotches cover his scalp, ironic proof that the cancer pills are working. "How about a few drops of Pear Essence, Dad?"

"Eh, what?"

"I can rub it on your head. You know, one of my flower essences to help restore a sense of peace in times of trauma."

"Pear-schmear, what's the difference?" Dad shifts on the bed, restless and distracted. "Sure, why not?"

Within minutes his discomfort vanishes—completely. He pats the area that only moments earlier had suffered blistering pain while a look of wariness bordering on shock replaces his distress. *Or is it disbelief that something non-allopathic might actually benefit him?* Herbs: I doubt that Dad ever used them in his life.

"Well, well. *Finally!* A testimonial from you for one of my products." My father's mood lightens and levity is restored.

Dad is in a state of grace. Many loved ones, including the members of two communities—Moshe's orthodox network and my spiritual family—are sending him daily prayers. The vehicle of this brutal disease that is both blessed and cursed renders him frail, limping, tiny, pale. As his life force withdraws from his body, my father seems more tender, childlike, and ultimately more receptive to that grace.

A most welcome sound sleep last night furthered my sense of well-being. *Finally*, I sigh, listening to the rhythm of my own breath as if through a doctor's stethoscope. Sustained by my spiritual teachings the joy is so deep, immense, intense that I wasn't at all certain if I'd even be able to sleep. Not so with the previous night at Tommy's. Perhaps I wasn't close enough to Dad with him downstairs and me upstairs. The *dharma* of caring for him is so strong that too much distance between us creates within me an almost physical discomfort.

I'm noticing a subtle and inward shift, either for me or for us both. I suspect the latter. These days with my father are a great honor. Not that it's easy. But it's getting more so as I begin to understand how the process of dying, much like living, is all about consciousness. The brilliance of Dad's soul is stepping forward, and I feel I'm being introduced to his essence for the first time. Together we've found a tear in the veil that separates this world from the hereafter to glimpse the astral realms. Home now to my father is where the angels sing.

I looked over yonder and what did I see,
Comin' for to carry me home.
A band of angels comin' after me,
Comin' for to carry me home.

Dad senses it too. Twice yesterday he commented on the peacefulness of his condominium. He seems happy in the sanctuary of his nest. That he can remain here is a great comfort to his five offspring.

Indeed, something *has* shifted. Dad's back to his customary joking and storytelling. One subject of much light-heartedness is the Tarceva-induced acne. Even with the distressing symptoms of severe facial pain (only his scalp responded to the Pear Essence), swollen ankles, and arthritis that has so cruelly attacked both of his legs, he seems more relaxed. Truly a lifetime of positive attitudes is sustaining him.

"I always told your mom that life was a game." Dad smiles his remarkable smile. "And she would say, 'Oh no, Aar. No, it isn't.' But I knew I was right."

To Dad, life has always been a game, and his teammates now are a band of angels.

Later that night in the pseudo-comfort of the guest room cluttered with mismatched furniture, I write to a friend at Ananda,
where many of us have taken spiritual names to reflect our spiritual core:

Dear Savitri,

I'm doing very well, thanks to our sacred path. My father
is on a roller coaster of horrific symptoms from the cancer IV
and daily pills. Why they call this "quality of life" is beyond my
understanding! Fortunately, Dad's always been a happy guy.
I've been helping out twenty-four-seven and for the most part
able to stay centered and joyful. That is my victory. I remind
myself of Yogananda's words: circumstances are neutral and
it's our interpretation of them that makes them seem either
happy or sad. Also helpful is his explanation of human nature—that we are all striving toward the same two goals: to be
happy and to be free from pain.

Please stay in touch.

Much love with prayers to you and your dear boy, and
appreciation for your prayers,

Lila

Hi, Lila,

Yes, I always wonder what that "quality of life" thing means.
I think the medical profession just plays into people's fear of
dying and makes big bucks in pumping poor souls with poison so

they can live just a tiny bit longer, but with a huge price.

What a world we live in! I do pray for you and your father and your whole family every day.

Savitri

Dear Savitri,

I completely agree.

The heartache of watching a loved one cling to and fight for this life as it slips from his grasp—what to say? I'm thinking of Swamiji's words, that whenever he sees people struggling, he thinks not of their present suffering, but of how great will be their joy when they find God and all suffering ends.

Your prayers are most dear.

Lila

A Seamstress's Lament

"I have to live now," Dad says at our card game that ends in a tie. He probably meant to say, "I have to lie down now."

My parent shuffles from the dining room to the bedroom while I watch to ensure he doesn't stumble or faint. It's as though I'm seeing his life pass before my eyes. Draped around his shoulders is the bathrobe I sewed for him in my teens that in years gone by served as a smoking jacket when he still lit his cigars and puffed on his pipes. Now he only chews on the pipe's plastic mouthpiece, a pungent odor of fine tobacco lingering in the pockets.

The cornflower blue polyester robe trimmed with a masculine Celtic-pattern is mid-calf length. *Were synthetic fabrics really once considered such a vast improvement over natural fibers?* No ironing, no wrinkles—and a dream come true for the busy homemaker! The robe is marked with the proud copyright of all my creations. A label unstitched on one end inside the back collar dangles like a broken tree limb declaring, *Fashioned by Linda Zaret.* The garment now hangs loosely on Dad's shrinking form.

Yet he wears it as stately as ever.

With a burst of adolescent pride, I cashed the paychecks from my first job to purchase a Singer sewing machine that punched the seams on the synthetic blue fabric. The needle's repetitive drone drowned out the hum of the television beyond the walls of my room. Many a post-homework evening was spent stitching Sixties styles with their short hem-line dresses and loose bell-bottom trousers. I was a budding seamstress.

Every day after school I worked at Dexter Davison Super-market, a sprawling Jewish grocery store near a busy intersection not far from where we lived. I would return home just past dinnertime. A scale girl's job earned me the minimum hourly wage of $1.40. My responsibilities included memorizing the long list of produce prices; weighing the bagged fruits and vegetables; and marking the cash total on the brown paper bags with a thick black crayon before stapling them closed.

I liked my job. A lot. Oh, how grown up I felt! It was fun to be efficient, greet customers, and as someone who actually cared about the produce, help make people's shopping experience more pleasant. You might even say I was good at my job, which is why getting fired after only six weeks left me devastated. Without any explanation whatsoever, I was simply let go.

One day, the metered ringing of the telephone interrupted my preparations for work. "Hello?"

"Is this Miss Zaret?"

"Yes. Who's calling?" The muscles of my fingers tensed in

response to the flat-toned voice pulsing through the receiver.

"It's the store manager," he said, peremptorily. "You don't have to come in today."

"Really, *what*?" My hand trembled. Dumbstruck and uncertain that I'd heard the words correctly or that they had been spoken in English, I asked, "Why?"

"We just have to let you go, that's all." The manager conveyed icily that the call had already ended.

"But *why*? There has to be a *reason*, you at *least* have to give me a reason. *Can't you tell me why?*"

"Please come by this week to pick up your final paycheck."

Click.

The reason for my job termination held no mystery to me. Nor did it to my friend, the other scale girl whose job security was not at risk.

I was fired for refusing to let the supervisor pinch me in the fruit section.

The assistant manager was a towering dark-haired man with several chins whose thick waist spilled over the edges of his stained apron like a pasty white-floured gravy. Buried beneath the flesh of his corpulent ring finger was a gold wedding band. Everything about the man was greasy and low. Instinct told me to stay as far away from him as possible.

My girlfriend kept her job. She also got pinched daily, somewhere in the aisles between the bright bins of apples and the two-for-one bags of ruby-red grapefruit.

New Sheriff in Town

"She's learning how to play. It's not easy for her. Your sister has a good vocabulary, Tommy, but she wanted to make a word with the letter *j* for only eleven points. *Eleven points!* Points-schmoints, whaddaya talkin' about?

"Who throws away a good letter like that?" Dad divulges to his youngest son the details of our latest Scrabble game.

"But she's coming along. We're working on it."

"Linda, I don't like the way you dress." My father speaks his mind with me freely, easily, and bluntly, sometimes too much so for my sensibilities.

Jackson's visit tonight grants me the freedom of a welcome break that also gives them some alone-time. *Maybe I can find an outfit that will be pleasing to Dad—something to wear for our lunches on Ventura Boulevard at Bamboo or his other favorite restaurants.* I return to the condominium mid-game with a dress that I find very much to my liking at a nearby department store. Something smart, classy, elegant-with-a-hint-of-vintage.

"Am I interrupting your game?" They *nosh* on a deli sandwich that Jackson brought with her.

"No, Dolly, of *course* not!" Dad counts his points while Jackson keeps score on their evenly matched volley of mental prowess, the lilting alto voice of Ella Fitzgerald wafting through the ether like a hazy trail of bar room smoke.

A perfect time to model my new dress while they're focused on the game board.

"Eh, I love it, Lin!" exclaims Jackson, the warmth of her Canadian accent affirming our camaraderie, her large eyes growing even bigger.

Dad glances up from his Scrabble letters. "Nice." He shifts his attention back to the board. "Will ya look at that? I just found a way to use the letter *x* on a triple-word square!" "But *Dad*. You didn't even *look* at me!" *Perhaps a three-quarter pivot on my toes will catch his attention.* "Do you really like my new dress, or are you just *saying* you like it?"

"Got some bad news for you gals." Dad's blustering Gabby Hayes accent hovers like a low fog over the Scrabble board.

"Eh, what, Zeke?" Jackson shifts in her seat.

"There's a new sheriff in town." Dad shares his trademark comment when taking the lead in a game, imitating the Western screen star who, ironically, is buried at a cemetery near his home.

The next morning, he's more forthcoming about my purchase. "Linda, I can't stand your new dress. It makes me want to vomit."

"Da-*aa*-ad, why didn't you tell me last night—*before* I cut off the price tag?"

"Don't *kvetch*. Don't you know you're supposed to wear clothes that make you look *younger*?" Then he adds more softly, "I can see I'll have to take you shopping."

"So, Dad, how's by you?" The tenderness in Moshe's voice softens an undertone of concern.

"Fine," says the parent. "But this afternoon I'll be doing even better. I'm taking my daughter to buy a new dress, we're going to Bloomingdale's."

Shopping for us children is one way that Dad wraps his love around us. This was something his own father never did; keeping food on the table was all my grandfather could manage.

Our pilgrimage to the mall is almost biblical with all these things about to be added unto me. We cross the boundary line into The Land of Retail. Dad swings open the tall glass doors of the department store with a single swagger, the new sheriff in town strutting through the rickety-hinged door of the saloon. An aura of slum-boy-turned-aristocrat fills the gigantic space. Dad's loafers of polished leather click on the shiny floor while I lag several steps behind, barely able to keep pace with him. The store's lighting mimics the softness of dawn promising hopes of perfect purchases to eager consumers. Lulled by the background music, we are mesmerized into an altered universe, meanwhile a sense of well-being replacing any lurking fears about spending perhaps too much money. The well-crafted ambiance dampens the dread of credit card bills once the present hypnosis wears thin, much like a short-lived dental anesthetic.

With a blend of respect and familiarity, Dad addresses the salesgirl in the men's cologne department. "Excuse me, Miss, can you direct us to the women's perfume section?" Joyfully he taps his fingers on the glass countertop to the rhythm of an internal song heard only by himself.

Next he approaches a young salesman at the men's shirts counter. "Sir, might you tell me where to find women's dresses? This is my daughter and I'm teaching her how to shop."

My father, who views everyone as a friend, often confides in perfect strangers as though they were next of kin—sometimes at the expense of his children who may find his comments not a little embarrassing.

Here at the sacred shrine of Bloomingdale's, my father buys the last dress he'll ever buy for me. It's chic, stylish, youthful. Compliments are always forthcoming on the special occasions when I wear it.

Just for the record, though, I also receive praise for the dress I bought for myself—from everybody, of course, except Dad.

MATZOH BALL SOUP FOREVER

A thick Russian accent journeyed with Dad's mother from the Motherland to Midwestern America. It remained with her throughout her life after immigrating from Gomel—a large city in Bellarus rumored to be named after a stream that flowed near the settlement land of its first immigrants—even though her command of the English language was more than passable. Many were the times when friends would ask her to translate their letters from Russian to English. Social by nature, she loved the liveliness of company in her living room with its worn floral-patterned sofas. Although diminutive in height, Bubbi Dora was, in spirit, a towering woman. And you listened when she spoke. She was in that respect just like my father.

"Your Bubbi's house, if it didn't smell like matzoh ball soup," Dad says, "it was gefilte fish. Or such a beet borscht. *Oy*, could she cook like nobody's business, your grandma."

I never met my grandfather. Phillip provided for a wife and seven children on the wages of a cabinetmaker, keeping them fed, clothed, and sheltered as the blackened pages of The Great

Depression unfurled. My Zayde had the finely chiseled features of an artisan. I never heard his voice, though I like to imagine it thickly varnished with a Russian accent embellished with a throaty resonance whose vowels, placed before a series of consonants, curled up like cats. Nor did I ever hear the crisp tapping of his cabinet-making tools. I would guess they clipped like my father's polished footsteps on tiled floors. The sepia-toned family photos portray my Zayde as a man with an intelligent forehead, an even nose, and thinly defined lips. His piercing eyes penetrate the faded paper with a glare that defies time as though gazing uninterruptedly into infinity.

The years between 1880 and 1920 saw an era in Russia unlike any other. People ran from the Czar, the communists, and the pogroms. With the Czar and his Bolchevik successors despising the Jews, bands of inebriated soldiers would pillage the Jewish villages. Humanity was falling apart at the seams. The greatest concentration of the Jewish community at that time settled in the Pale of White Russia, a focal point for the largest Jewish immigration in world history. Millions of Jews were to land on the shores of America.

Bubbi Dora was one of them. The year 1910 marked her arrival in Chicago as a married woman while cousin after cousin, totaling dozens of relatives, would be landing for many years to come. Bubbi, as one relative was quoted as saying, "made it her business to welcome everyone." Doors in her home were removed from their hinges and fashioned into beds at night to accommodate the immigrants, escaping in fear for their lives from the brutal pogroms with only the shirts on their backs.

With great animation and often, Dad will tell The Convulsions Story.

The familiar scent of beet borscht in a beef broth dusted with sugar and salt emanated in waves from the kitchen. Dinner would soon be served. Not yet a year old, the young Aaron had fallen ill with a high fever, sweats, and convulsions. Bubbi Dora tried all that could be done to lower his temperature.

"If this happens again," the doctor said to the mother who stood in the steamy shadows of the kitchen, twisting the knuckles of her worn hands together, "don't call me. Call the rabbi. There's nothing more I can do for your boy."

When Aaron again grew ill and febrile, the rabbi was called. Cradling the child in his arms, he walked into the bedroom, closed the door with the heel of his shoe, and muttered prayers under his breath in fervent Hebrew that found their way through the graying strands of his beard.

At last the rabbi emerged, handing the boy child to my Bubbi. "Your son will be fine." He prophesied this news with the awed assurance of one whose prayers have been answered.

"What's more, he shall live to have his own children."

"And what were my toys," Dad says, "growing up in the slums of Chicago? A ball, a stick, and a deck of cards." So shares my father on this dreamlike weekend morning.

Soon he too, just like his own father, will gaze from photographs on the wall in hallways that ring with Sabbath laughter to touch the unborn generations of his lineage.

Lunchtime at the Burbank Boulevard condominium is enlivened with the arrival of Noah and Tommy. My brother looks like several movie actors rolled into one. The graceful sport of tennis that crystallizes the symphony of muscle strength and hand/eye coordination has lavished on him a lithe agility of body and mind. Tom moves like a dancer. He exudes the nobility of one equally at ease at a tennis court and a court of law. He plops a heavy shopping bag on the kitchen counter like a well-placed tennis ball that barely grazes the net. We are about to feast. The makeshift meal of deli treats from the local health food store offers something for everyone, including sliced chicken for Dad and veggies for Sis. Tommy prepares a plate for his son.

My father's aura expands whenever Noah visits. His youngest grandson answers each question with a simple tickling brilliance.

"Noah," Dad asks, "are you going to save your Legos for your own son?"

"Probably not. I don't think I'll have children," he replies matter-of-factly between bites of a cheese sandwich.

"Oh, and why's that?"

"Because, Zayde, I'm having trouble finding a girlfriend."

"Do you think that might change someday?"

"I doubt it. I've learned a few things in my five years. You know," Noah tells Tommy about their recent basketball game, "I could have beat you when I was in my prime."

Moshe, Bracha, Chana, and Sara bolt through the hallway, aglow with the blessings of yesterday's Sabbath, the narrow corridor amplifying their enthusiasm. I set three kinds of rugelach on the coffee table—apricot, raisin, and cinnamon walnut—after compacting stacks of outdated magazines to clear space for the paper plates, since keeping kosher means they cannot eat from our dinnerware.

Sara speaks privately with her grandfather in the tiny dining room, their profiles haloed in gold by the sunlight streaming in from the courtyard. Zayde loves his girls with tenderness and protectiveness, his boys with pride and appreciation. Moshe's youngest child is in her late teens. Nearly of marrying age, she inherited her Bubbi's keen insights into human nature, and the gracefulness of her hands—silky, lithe, swanlike. Sara's thick coal-black hair is so like my mother's in her youth. Now it can fall freely into her eyes. Once she marries, it will be covered in public by a wig or a scarf for the remainder of her life, as dictated by Jewish law that defines the modest behavior of an espoused orthodox Jewish woman.

This moment by which other moments are measured is filled with a timeless love that spans beyond incarnations.

The front door closes after the last family member leaves. Dad tells me the story of taking his beloved cat to the veterinary hospital for treatment many years ago. "I opened the car door and Special Kitty escaped." His eyes are downcast and hollow.

"I called to her for hours but I never saw her again." Ever a lover of animals, still he never replaced her with another cat.

Taped to Dad's refrigerator door calendar are marked the watering days for his one and only houseplant. The rhododendron on the coffee table may be the first plant he's ever owned. My wish is to see everyone in the family receive a cutting from this plant, watered with tenderness by their Zayde, that it may flourish throughout the years as a reminder of his vitality—a desire that somehow never manifested, as no one expressed interest in the idea. My own cutting now sits on my kitchen counter in a white ceramic pot. It thrives with life force and color.

Phil and Patty are next to visit. My brother's salt-and-pepper goatee might look garish on other chins but on his, it has found a handsome home on the contours of his strong-boned face. With a sweeping motion, Patty kisses the top of her father-in-law's head and takes her place beside him. Dad is laying horizontal on the couch. His legs are propped up on a pillow. A clot in his left thigh could prove fatal if the blood-thinning medication that he injects twice daily into his abdomen fails to dissolve it. Though he now tires easily, seeing his children has an immediate positive effect on his overall energy.

Each moment lived is a moment treasured.

"*Nu*, Dad, I'm in a pinch here, can ya give me some advice?" Moshe asks over the phone. "I need a million-dollar donation for our new UCLA campus center. The donor, he gets to have a plaque posted in honor of his parents. Ya gotta help me out, Dad, I'm telling you." Moshe pronounces the *ing* gerund as *ink*. "A potential donor came forward but he only offered half a million."

One of my-brother-the-rabbi's outreach programs is Ashrainu; the other is called J.A.M. The Jewish Awareness Movement is an on-campus student-run club at the University of California, Los Angeles that provides educational and experiential opportunities for Jewish students to "learn and grow Jewishly and meet other Jewish students." One suggested activity in my rabbi brother's own writing on his website is to join a traditional Sabbath dinner with a family that provides "chicken soup; gefilte fish; conversation with other university students; a chance to learn more about Judaism; and cute children jumping all over you."

"So Dad, what to do? What does your business wisdom say here?"

"Hold out for the full million, Sonny." Dad seems patently pleased to be actively involved in his son's life. "Million-shmillion, what's the difference? Maybe the guy can have a change of heart." Dad loves recreating this story about the business advice he gave to Moshe. Thinly hidden within his reply is the pride that his son has asked for his counsel.

Scoring over four hundred points in our first Scrabble game of the day is, for Dad, a glorious win. As for me, I can't seem to focus. I play my letters stupidly and lose badly. It happens, he would say. The game affirms to Dad that his mind is as sharp as ever. All is right in his world with his life still under his control. Yet he has the gall to ask me to check Scrabble words that patently don't exist? When I ask him to do likewise for me, my reward is a sharp reprimand. The double standard, it seems, will never end.

Two Vicodin tablets at last dull Dad's pain, making him woozy. I walk him to bed, his gait uncertain but determined. There is nothing easy about helping someone who doesn't want to be helped, but I know his wishes are to be respected. Each step affirms that he shuns his loss of independence. Witnessing his battle to remain with his loved ones hastens me in my spiritual practices, to go longer and deeper in my meditations, to "die daily" to life's transient ups and downs, and to strive to "go no more out,"—that is, to not be forced by one's attachments to this world to reincarnate yet again into the illusive cycle of birth and death.

Surely my father has earned the right to cling to whatever shreds of autonomy still linger in his shrinking world—a world in which he's struggling with all his will to remain

Keeping Chicago Great

Thursday, September 21, 1950: Unedited article in an Illinois newspaper.

Keeping Chicago Great: 4 Brothers' Art Studio Run Into Big Business.

When four brothers get together to run a little business, it kind of gets special attention. The Zaret boys, sons of a cabinet-maker, lived at 1642 S. Homan Avenue.

Frank Zaret started the Alba Arts Studios four years ago with two sculptors as assistants. He named the business— Alba—after one of the partner's wife (sic), made a line of art creations, hand cast in metal, for display of flowers. His slogan: "the best in art is none too good for the display of flowers."

Two years ago his brothers came into the business. Morris, 33, is office manager, used to be traffic manager of a truck line. Mitchell, 27, graduate of Illinois Tech, is production manager, and Zeke, 23, is sales manager.

With eight employees—and they expect to have 20 by

Christmas—the brothers carry on in a second floor loft at 1840 S. Michigan with 5,000 square feet.

Their business began to jump when they introduced a novelty called "Timelite"—it is an artistically constructed combination electric clock and cigarette lighter in the form of a desk telephone. The telephone dial is an electric clock. The lighter is operated by pushing a button with your thumb as you hold up the "receiver" to "talk." It's a clever gadget.

Frank says he was interested in art since he was 9 years old. He studied with Todros Geller, Samuel Ostrowsky and Maurice Ritman until he was 17. Then he went to a WPA sculpture school, was more than ever convinced . . . Institute three nights a week continuing his studies of design.

He told me art is a thing that doesn't stand still, you have to keep up your studies to get ideas of new products and new methods.

When the boys get an idea they design it in clay, then cast it in plaster, then make a plaster shell and send it to a foundry where it is cast in bronze or steel. Mass production begins when the castings are sent to a foundry where they pour a lower melting-point metal into the molds.

The greatest thing about Chicago, said Frank, is the fine help they have had from casting plants and foundrymen who took an interest in seeing the little first get started.

"There isn't anything like it anywhere," he said.

An original investment of $8,000 has grown in 4 years to over $50,000; sales which totaled $58,000 in the year ended Aug. 32, 1949, were $127,000 in the year ended Aug. 31, 1950.

Chicago has more potentialities for product development than any other place, said Frank, due to its marvelous supplies and technical helps.

Pretzels, Pipes, and Inner Peace

Homesickness sits like undigested food in the pit of my stomach. I want to fly home. It feels like I've been in Los Angeles forever, and I miss my life. The thrill of easier access to shopping malls and bric-a-brac stores has outworn its welcome. I miss my spiritual family's heartfelt camaraderie, in Sanskrit called *satsang*. True, my work is carrying on reasonably well without me as it usually does in my absence.

Should I stay or go?

I've been asking myself this question for several days. Dad could conceivably manage safely on his own, though not as well as when I'm here. Today the answer comes. This is a frightening time for him, strong though he is. Paramount is having someone close by to hold him in the light and to support his good humor. Loading laundry and emptying the dishwasher are secondary tasks to my truer purpose in remaining: This is our genuine "quality time." It's not about the cards or the Scrabble or that he's still winning at games. It's about having a family member close by to help nourish his soul in its transition from this world, this body, this incarnation. My truer job description—that of spiritual midwife—is to assist with his birth into the astral world.

Cancer. A disease both blessed and brutal that allows my father a symptom-free time to assess his life and disassociate himself as best he can from any ties to this world. Meanwhile it provides a period of various pains and treatments to free his soul and help him leave this incarnation with less karmic baggage.

"You're the one in the trenches, Sis," brother Jackie tells me, "catching the storm of what Dad's body can't fight off." Meaning his intermittent grumpiness and binges of short temper. Yet his vacillating moods are affecting me less sharply all the time.

Whatever he's working through within himself, God only knows.

"My food is starting to taste funny," Dad says at our gin game where he beats me mercilessly. "When I drink orange juice—my favorite brand, Linnie, with the chunks of pulp—it tastes 'off.' And I feel hazy today. There's a film over my mental processes."

Even though Dad is chronically and profoundly tired, we're having a grand celebration. His live-in, half-decent game player just beat him in Scrabble. My winnings are not something that happen regularly, though often enough to provide him with a pittance of competition and an enjoyable challenge.

"Many months before my diagnosis, I knew something in my body was wrong."

"Oh? How could you tell?"

"My upper lip sometimes broke out in a sweat and that's not

right. Sweetie, what a good life it's been." And what a good attitude he's modeling. While the cancer symptoms are still under his control, my father is lording it over his life.

"Let's go to Jackson's on Magnolia." Dad elongates the second syllable of the street name like a child playing with his food.

Once there, we let ourselves in through the parking garage door. My parent reclines on a lounge chair beside the pool as I begin my laps. The altered embryonic universe of the water surrounds me, the ripples from my strokes tapping their knuckles against the submerged tiles that line the pool. The mid-afternoon sun hovers above our shoulders. At half-mast, it softens the poolside shadows, the warm Santa Ana winds whipping through the tall wooden fencing. My father's enrapt attention pivots toward his pocket-sized electronic gadget for a game of blackjack. It's not until we leave that Dad admits to being severely chilled.

"Why didn't you say something earlier, Pops? You could've stayed inside where it's warm!" *Why? Because like some majestic animal in the wild, any display of weakness might presage his annihilation.*

Dad answers and averts my question in a wordless breath.

"Linda, you're a bad swimmer."

The tangled Los Angeles freeway looks like hair needing to be combed. "You know, Dad," I say on the drive home from Jackson's pool, "out of respect I always dress orthodox around Moshe." The modest garb befitting a Jewess is defined by high necklines, low hemlines, and arms covered below the elbow.

"That's because you're orthodox at heart," he says firmly. "You're an orthodox Jew, you know."

Yes. I'm also orthodox Hindu, and God forbid, Christian. Orthodox as I understand it means a deep commitment to one's spiritual life.

Perfumed in the dearness of friendship coupled with her background in nursing, Sharon is a godsend with all the answers to my questions.

"I'm not trying—to be morbid, Sharon—I just want to get—a handle on what's going on." My sentences are broken by several short breaths, climbing and descending the three floors in the stairwell across the courtyard from my father's condominium. "What—does it mean—that Dad's ankles—are swollen up—like balloons? That he—may be—passing soon?"

"It could be a few weeks. Based on those symptoms, perhaps the liver's shutting down."

"The tests show—a blood clot."

"Oh then, no. As your dad's time draws closer, he'll start to lose interest in outer activities. This is the soul's process of withdrawing from this world. Ask yourself each morning if you should be there, that's the way to find an answer. *Lila, you know what to do.*"

I pause on the steps, winded and energized. "Was it right to tell him what I've learned about the symptoms as the cancer progresses? Maybe I shouldn't have said anything."

"Yes, it was right. Because he asked. Information can strengthen him, and he can prepare himself and feel empowered by it."

Good. Because I really don't know what I'm doing or how to help Dad leave this life he so cherishes. "Okay, got it." Still breathing hard, I reflect on these treasured breaths that keep me in this world. "The next morning—my father blasted me, Sharon—with complete rage. Was his anger—directed at me?"

"I think his love and closeness to you, Lila, allowed him to vent his fear-based anger. That doesn't make it right. But it's a fear response. He feels safe enough with you to be angry, and he knows you won't stop loving him because of it."

"Oh—makes sense. Interesting you'd say that. I talked with my-brother-the-doctor Phil just last night about the involuntary subconscious function of the nervous system—the autonomic flight-fight response."

"You know, Lila, I have a great fear of heights. Once while helping Tom replace shingles on our roof, I got very, very angry! It really surprised me."

Dad has just laid down for a nap. With the bedroom door open, I peek in to check on him. The arms of divine slumber enfold him more often now as his various bodily systems slacken. His hair, tousled white and still thick, is outlined against the stacked pillows like a penciled line drawing. Laying on his back with his knees bent and his mouth open, he seems to be living more in Heaven than in this world.

As your dad's time draws closer, he'll start to lose interest in outer activities. This is the soul's process of withdrawing from this world.

Dad is most concerned with maintaining his sense of control. Hence according to his strict instructions, I put away the dishes and put up the laundry. His ability to talk about his symptoms and my willingness to give feedback help him to remain in charge of his life, conducting business as usual. Together we're a team. We can avert any sense of alarm. Though he might just thoroughly beat me in cards. This is a powerful time for me as well as for my father.

Loneliness wraps itself around me like an awkward cloak. Even so if I were back home, I know I'd want to be here. Maybe now is exactly when my father needs me. Maybe this is exactly where I'm supposed to be. Seeing him tap into the soul qualities that he expresses with such exuberance consoles me. Indeed his songs, dances, and stories fortify him.

Today is my baby brother's birthday. Tommy Boy, our little rug rat, turns forty-nine today. This slang figure of speech for a young child not yet ready for school may not be the most endearing term, but such are the odd ways of family.

Dad and I have a talk this morning that's light, connective, part of our daily routine. He tells me whatever stories strike his fancy, sharing the wisdom he's gleaned from his life experiences. He plays with his sentences, each word a different-flavored jellybean. Never will my father run out of stories. Interspersed in his monologue are some of his favorite sayings: "You got that right." "You can say *that* again." "Life is short." "Do a good job." And the one previously mentioned that irks me and everybody else each time he says it: "You're serious? I'm Roebuck!"

My father is a complex person.

He changes his shirts and his shoes several times a day to suit his comfort and match his moods. The bedroom closet bulges with high-quality cotton dress shirts and leather shoes. Such clothing is quite a step up for the little slum-raised youngster who wore his brothers' hand-me-downs until they frayed beyond recognition.

Yet Dad's condominium has declined into shambles.

The paint on the walls is dirty and scuffed, a plastic panel in the kitchen ceiling has long since caved in, and neither the heating nor the air conditioning work. Fortunately, Phil convinced him to fix the cooling system before the grueling summer heat began to laminate the streets of North Hollywood. Then there are the pathetically threadbare bathroom towels half a century old. This, I know for a fact because I grew up with them. Their outdated color combinations are a little hard on the eye—brown, lime green, burnt orange? *Whoever rendered this mishmash of a color palette: what are they, nuts?*

I reach into the refrigerator to store a half-full can of soup that I've neatly covered with aluminum foil. Dad walks up behind me. He looks over my shoulder and says with horrified scrutiny,

"Oh, *no-o.* We don't do that here." I am reprimanded with a force-fulness reserved for someone who has just broken several of the Ten Commandments and will soon be receiving a stern smiting from God Himself.

"But Da-ad. You can't be—I mean—"

An exposed light bulb in the collapsed ceiling overhead flickers with delight at the absurdity of our argument.

"*That,*" he says peremptorily," goes in a plastic container."

If an Eleventh Commandment were to exist, it might read: *Thou shalt not covereth the remains of a can of soup with foil amidst the abundance of plastic containers in which to storeth thy leftovers.*

And *that,* as brother Jackie would say, *is that.*

How Dad grieves relinquishing his pipes and fine cigars! Many are the nights at the dining table when he gnaws instead on a low-salt pretzel. Though now he's returned to his cigars, always unlit, seeking an inner peace from the altered breathing that accompanies the healthless act of smoking. Even worse, he's commenced the habit of chewing tobacco. Disgusting to the point of nauseating me, Sharon would say it shows he's comfortable enough with me to chew and spit in my presence without any shame or pretense. An odd testimony to our closeness! Sometimes I wish there *were* a sense of shame or pretense so he'd quit the habit.

Why bother to care for a perishing body or proper decorum? What can one say in objection to someone who knows he's leaving this world and no longer needs to abide by its rules? *Dad, that's not good for your health? Dad, that's a vile habit?*

Or: Dad, be joyful in whatever ways help you to feel the touch of God's hand.

"Linnie," my father asks with a concerned frown, "how do I look to you?" The balance weights on the upright doctor's scale in his bedroom reveal a further loss of two pounds.

"How do *you* think you look?" The intellectual Jewish strategy of answering a question with a question never fails to disarm and deflect. "Well, your cheeks have color. Dad, you're a real cutie."

"Whaddaya talkin' about?" He stretches the syllables of his run-together words into song lyrics and breaks into a light two-step. "A little *noshing* here, a little *noshing* there. What's—not—to *nosh*?" My father beams the searchlight of his famous smile in which is captured his essence, to ignite joy within the hearts of his audience. Like the fabled Cheshire cat, he *is* that smile.

"I'm afraid, Sister, because I don't have any symptoms yet."

"*Re-ally?*" His comment puzzles me. He's managed well this far, as I see it, even while harboring a fear of what lies ahead. "Dad—it looks to me like all you've *had* are symptoms!"

A sacred journey to Bloomie's to shop for Tommy's birthday present is our plan for the afternoon. Since he likes to dress casually after spending his court days in a business suit, Dad shops for tee-shirts for his youngest child. One he rejects as too cheap; another, too costly. I mean, four hundred dollars for a *tee-shirt? Are you serious? No, I'm Roebuck.*

Dad takes his time perusing colors, textures, sizes. Who can know his thoughts? *Perhaps that when he's in Heaven, he wants his boy to be well groomed?* Seeing Dad pick out Tommy's presents with such tender care reminds me of sitting *shiva* for Mom seven years ago. A tiny rabbi, whose skin tone radiated the delicacy of a China tea set, sat folded in the far corner of Moshe's living room, a mere wisp of a man with a cascading beard. An aura of dearness wrapped around him like a *tallis* that had witnessed many prayer sessions. In a voice aged, wise, and heavily accented from the British Isles, he counseled my father: "Now that your wife is gone, both a father and a mother to your children you'll have to be."

Seeing Dad shop for Tommy, I'm reminded of the rabbi's prophetic words—*because that's exactly what he's doing.*

The sun pouts in the mid-afternoon sky. The colorless heat of a summer's day illuminates the strip mall's string of shops—a video store, a dry cleaners, a kosher bakery, and a market-under-new-management-turned-kosher, running a sale on all *traif* foods.

Time to take a break, I'm thinking, for a little pampering and self-care. The beauty salon across the street is a place of pilgrimage where, for a small fee, women can exit the shrine more beautiful than when they first entered. Perhaps some highlights streaked through my hair will create a worthy diversion? Eva the hairdresser preens herself in front of the mirror on a break between customers, freshening her lipstick and blotting her newly brightened mouth on a tissue. As a foreigner who's not so hot with the English language, maybe she doesn't understand my request since I seem to be the only person in the shop who doesn't speak Armenian.

Oh, drat. My hair turns out a little racier than I'd like. But I figure I'll get used to it in time. Being so distracted with Dad these days, even a spiked purple Mohawk wouldn't much faze me.

"*Nu*, Dad, what do you think?" I turn full-circle to show off my new do from all angles. The *Los Angeles Times* floats across the bed covers, immersed in small drifts of clipped grocery coupons.

"Put your hair up in a pony tail so I can't see it." Aaron returns his attention to the sports page.

I guess that means he's not so crazy about it.

On the Escalator to
Higher Realms

If my father's life were made into a movie, the actor who plays
him would have to be both handsome and complex.

The details one remembers about a loved one can be so varied—
trivial, poignant, touching, inspiring. Silly stories. Some mean-
ingless, some significant, all holding special memories. It's as
though my own life is flashing before my eyes these days in uni-
son with what I imagine to be happening for Dad.

When I was a child before Moshe and Tommy were born,
we vacationed in Michiana, a beachside resort bordering south-
western Michigan and northern Indiana. Like a land that time
forget, the southern town of Harbor County displayed street
names of Native American Indians to honor them as its earliest
residents. There we visited our distant relatives' rustic log cabin hidden within a patch of woods. In the late afternoon when
the heat would begin to abate, cousins and siblings picked wild
blueberries on the land, eating most of them before they clinked
their way into our metal buckets, our mouths stained blue from

the tart juice. Auntie Mamie baked pies from whatever fruit remained. Many little shins were scratched from the low thorns, our worthy battle scars for retrieving our "berried treasure."

Mom, Dad and the five of us kids vacationed at the nearby Hilltop Motel with a swimming pool that was pure magic for us. Whenever anyone complained to Dad about getting bitten by mosquitoes, his response was always the same, neither practical nor helpful.

"Bite 'em back."

Brothers Phil and Jackie remember the long car rides when in true sibling fashion we fought over the window seats. Who wanted to be flanked on both sides by the sibs when anarchy could erupt at any moment onto the trapped middle child?

Aaron had his own style of driving. He would shift into reverse and turn the steering wheel, thumping and spinning it simultaneously with a smooth and never jerky movement. The favorite place to sit was by the window behind Dad which always managed to be my seat, being The Big Sister.

Spending the night at Tommy's allowed Dad to join the Friday night poker game with his buddies and three of his sons—everyone but Moshe, who was horrified time and again to hear how his father spent the sacred Sabbath hours. Dad has always acted as though he owns the world with his own set of rules about how to live in it, meaning that he'll play poker on Friday nights if it pleases him.

"Hey, Sis, nice racing stripes!" Tommy snaps, inspecting the highlights in my hair as he maneuvers his BMW convertible into the garage.

"Hi there, bro!" I shout over my shoulder, huffing too hard on the treadmill to conjure a more clever response. "Just remember when you were a kid who washed your dishes!"

The weekend bathing suit sale at Macy's delays our homecoming from Tommy's, much to the delight of Dad and his daughter. "Pick out two suits, Linda, not one. I want you to have two." My father—quieter now and less chatty with the store personnel—sits outside the fitting room hallway more patiently than I've ever remembered him. "Wear them in the best of health," he says on the escalator that delivers us from higher realms down to the parking lot, adding with choked emotion, "You only live once."

On the drive home, I ask him, "So Dad, tell me—do you believe in Judaic law?"

"Of course, Dolly! Why?"

"Well, I was just thinking you might want to talk to Moshe about how Judaism honors reincarnation. You're not going to hang out in Heaven for infinity, you know! You'll be coming back to this world."

I'm not sure how my parent takes this news—or if he takes it at all. I suspect it's somehow comforting to him. At least it seems to ease his sense of finality about leaving this life he savors with such passion. Later through my-brother-the-rabbi, I will learn that the Judaic acceptance of reincarnation can be found in the tenth chapter of the Talmud Sanhedrin.

"And Dad?"

"Yes, sweetie?" He eyes the current gas prices as we drive past the corner station. With one hand on the wheel I reach out to touch his arm, comforted to feel he's still in this world, still beside me, and to reassure him through this simple gesture that I will stay with him until his last breath. *God willing.* Little did I know God had other plans in mind.

"Remember how you said recently you feel you got this disease because God's testing your strength?" My voice muffles tentatively in the upholstered confines of the car.

"So, *nu?*" Dad adjusts the unwieldy seat belt that seems to have suddenly wrenched itself too tightly across his chest.

"Well," I begin sheepishly, not at all certain how to phrase my thoughts in terms that he might accept or at least consider. Metaphysical talks with my father lead us into uncharted territory. "I agree completely. With *part* of what you said. It does seem that you're being tested, but I'm thinking it might also have something to do with the giving and receiving of love."

"I need to be an example of strength to my children." Dad continues as though I haven't spoken. The traffic light shifts to green and we make a left-hand turn from Riverside onto Woodman.

"*Dad.* You're one of the strongest people I know! If *I* can know that, don't you think *God* knows it too?"

He replies with an awkward pause. Never do we speak deeply of spirituality, especially after my exodus from formal religion. Dad seems patently uncomfortable with the subject. If we were at home, this is exactly when he'd be turning on the television to disappear into the thick mist of a baseball game.

Monday, September 15, 2008

My father has disappeared into the ether and my spiritual family voicemailed their support in the wake of his absence.

"Lila, I just got your message. Thank you for letting me know. It seems like it's all been a big cosmic setup to let your dad pass when you weren't there. I think there might have been something holding him back for whatever reasons. I know it must be sad in many ways that it had to happen like this, but sometimes in families things go this way because of past karma being all intricately mixed in with people's familial involvement with each other. So I'll tell my husband now; he just finished meditating. We'll say some prayers. I guess you'll be leaving here pretty quickly to get back to Los Angeles. Lots of blessings and love, talk to you later."

"Hi, Lila, I was just thinking about your dad a lot yesterday, the day before he passed. I'm very happy for you. I think he was ready to go. It seemed like he felt that way. I can't express this enough. So anyway, bless you. I'm happy for you that things turned out as well as they did for you. And for him. Surely he couldn't help but go to a higher realm into more joy. He must be very happy. Okay, sweetie, if there's going to be a memorial service, let me know. I'd love to come."

"I had such a strong feeling yesterday when you were talking about your dad that he was going to pass really soon. I'm a little surprised it was *this* soon, but I thought it would be the next forty-eight hours or less. I knew it wouldn't be much longer. What a blessing his passing was. Usually a person can't leave this world when a really close relative is there—the person trying to get out, can't. Your father has passed on such an auspicious weekend while we celebrate Swami's sixtieth anniversary of discipleship to Yogananda. He really chose well. He is now with God, truly (crying). Indeed, your father's very blessed to have you as a daughter (crying), so God bless and I'll see you later. Bye bye."

"Lila, we got your message about your father passing. That's a relief that you were able to go and be with him. That's a great gift to him, I'm sure, in these last few weeks. So we did pray for you and his soul and your family, and of course we'd be happy to do a memorial service when the timing works out for you. You'll be in our prayers now but I think as you say, his journey's begun and he's done with the confines of his physical body. God bless you, dear friend."

Dear Nalini,

Amazing story about my father's passing, isn't it? Interestingly enough, it especially touched my rabbi brother's heart since Jewish orthodoxy says that the soul leaves through the ground, which is exactly the position in which my brother found him, seated upright.

I'd like to think that Dad's way of passing sprung from his superconscious rather than subconscious state, that he was divinely and intuitively guided. These subtle truths I could never discuss with him, especially since he told me on the escalator at Bloomingdale's that we only have one life to live! When I sited the orthodoxy's long-buried acknowledgement of reincarnation, he still seemed to resist the idea.

Yet it all transpired perfectly.

About keeping himself minimally medicated: it drove us all crazy to see him so weakened and in pain. Even so, this was Dad's wish. His body was remarkably strong and could tolerate a barrage of drugs that I know without a doubt would have killed me. His fierce non-negotiable demand was to be given only what he was willing to take and no more. I watched hospice try repeatedly to push all kinds of meds on him as he declined—for insomnia, anxiety, depression—all to no avail. Their approach distressed me but at least it was well-intentioned. Of course they were no match for Dad!

In a sense, it was a win-win situation for him because he did indeed stay conscious and, to his satisfaction, in complete control to the very end.

In divine friendship,

Lila

A Sugar-coated Childhood

No one gave Aaron instructions on how to be a father. I was the guinea pig—his first born, raised by a manual. Unfortunately, it was the wrong one for my delicate temperament.

"*Oy vey*, pick her up and rock her," said my grandmother.

"Let her cry," said my mother.

"Stop that crying right this instant!" shouted my father.

It's said when a baby is born, the baby cries and everyone laughs; and when a person dies, he laughs while everyone else cries. Why did I cry so much? Colic, and knowing on some level that this wouldn't be the easiest of incarnations. You might say as far as tests go, I hit the ground running. Aside from being the ugliest baby Aaron had ever seen, by his own admission—and surely sensing on some level how he felt—I was raised as a newborn on canned baby formulas. An undetected thyroid condition rendered my mother unable to breastfeed. Thus my first meals of processed baby formulas were laced with refined white sugar.

They may as well have fed me intravenous candy bars. Or as

my Russian-Jewish grandmother used to say, figures of speech
in the English language not being her forte, "That's the way the
cookie bounces."

Aaron's Parents and Siblings

Dora with Aaron,
Her Youngest of
Seven Children

Five Brothers, 1942 (in ascending age, Dad first)

The Graduate

Enlisted Navy Men (Dad, second row, eighth from left)

Navy Zeke (left) with
Buddy Vern

Navy Zeke

Navy Zeke,
Smiling
Through

Honorable Naval
Discharge

My Mother

*Aaron's Alba Arts
Business Card*

Alba Arts Studio Wares

*Mom (back row, second to left),
High School Swim Team*

*Groom and Bride,
Aaron and Harriet*

Dad at the Michiana Beach

Harriet, the Backstroke Goddess

Mom Just Married

Aaron Always Joking

Newlyweds Harriet and Aaron

Tennis Dad and Mom with Jackie and Tommy

Salesman Zeke with Pipe

The Zaret Dynasty

Refrigerator Photo, Moshe's Back Stairs

Refrigerator Photo, Dad with Grandkids

Our Family Shortly Before Mom Passed

Last Passover, with Chana and Schmuel

Jackson and Dad

Phil Fixing CD Player

*Last Birthday with Dad
at Stanleys*

Working Out With Friends on a Caretaking Break

*Dad's Sketch of Special Kitty
on a Shirt Cardboard*

*Coupons Clipped
by Dad*

Dad

Gravestones of Dad with Mom

THE BROTHERS FOUR

D*earest Brothers,*

How are all you guys doing? It's been wonderful to see us getting closer through our care of Dad. Once I leave again, he'll be on his own, without a round-the-clock family member here. With a little extra attention on everyone's part, you can all fill in the gaps.

Here are some notes to supplement our scheduling. Can each of you let me know ASAP when you can visit Dad so I can get a calendar out to everyone?

1. *This Friday, Jackson returns from visiting family in Canada. She's great company for Dad, and he loves her dearly. Still, she's not on the schedule because Dad told me that he doesn't want her bothered unless she wants to visit of her own accord because she works full-time and cares for her mother on weekends.*

2. *When it's your appointed day (any time is fine, whatever works best for you), please call Dad or leave a voicemail to give him notice about when you can stop by. It will help him plan his time especially if Jackson is coming to visit.*

3. *If you can't make it on that day, please switch with someone so Dad's not left alone. There can be errands he needs taken care of that he won't mention by phone.*

4. *Calling him just to say hi is always nice. I can tell he appreciates this—but this doesn't replace your visit. Don't worry: you won't bother him if he's sleeping because the bedroom phone ringer is turned off.*

5. *Guys, Dad throws out LOTS of food so if you bring anything, it can be a meal or two but not more. Low-sodium is best.*

6. *Feel free to stay for fifteen minutes, half an hour, or longer. It's nice to eat with him. Company at mealtimes naturally encourages him to eat bigger portions. He does best not being pushed or nagged to eat more than he wants, so the energy stays light and supportive for him. Most of all, according to Drs. Phil and Beckwitz, he needs to DRINK and stay hydrated.*

7. *It's fine to let Dad fix his own food and clean up afterwards if he wants to. The exercise is good for him and lets him know he's still okay and independent. In other words, he doesn't care to be babied. If he needs something done, he'll let you know. "Sonny, get me a glass of chocolate milk. No, in the tall glass. No, about three-quarters full and the rest, regular milk."*

8. *What to do when you're here with him? Have fun! Play Scrabble or cards, watch baseball or basketball, or the ultimate: take him shopping at Ralphs which he loves!*

9. *When you take Dad out, he's pretty good about knowing if he needs to use the walker for support. If you see him looking shaky, just take it along and tell him it will be in the trunk if he needs it.*

10. *What's important is to check in with him and see how he's doing and if he needs anything—being aware that he might not tell you. It's that simple. Also I've found this time with Dad is deeply bonding. It's been a great gift for me and I know it will be for you guys as well.*

11. *One day recently, he was concerned about his appearance and disturbed about his weight loss and poor coloring. If he looks tired or pale, it helps to keep his spirits up if you say something positive. But don't lie to him either. You know Dad—he'll see right through you before you can even speak the words.*

12. *He likes to have family visit. Although he's cordial to Victor, he's not at all thrilled about having hired help. My sense is that Dad sees him as a symbol of his loss of independence and the progression of the disease. He's expressed he wants to have Victor's help as little as possible. He doesn't even want him on Fridays at this point (Liz, this is something you'll want to work with—either Tommy can bring him over to your place or ?).*

13. *Sisters-in-law and grandchildren who drive are most welcome to pitch in!*

14. *I've left Dad a calendar with his appointments for the next month that has all his doctors' phone numbers. (Moshe, are you still going to D.C. next week? Let me know.)*

15. *Guys, how about keeping this organizational thing a secret? I think Dad would appreciate our spontaneity, not our scheduling.*

16. *Tommy asked today when I'll be coming back. The answer: at this point, I don't know. Here at home, I'm getting my business in order and will return when needed, which may also be the time for hospice to step in with their hour-long visits to attend to Dad's medical and bathing needs.*

17. *Shall we do our conference calls with him on Monday nights at 8 p.m.? He loved the last one.*

18. *Since I'll be out of the loop, I'll be phoning you guys to hear how Dad's doing. When I call him to say hi, he always puts on a brave front for my benefit. It's just who he is. I think until his last breath, he'll be protecting me. He's well-intentioned, yes—but credible, no.*

Most of all, Dad's in a really good place with what's happening to him. Sometimes he wants to talk about what he's going through—what he's feeling, what's shifting in his body—and sometimes not. You'll get the hang of it. We may not know this disease, but we do know our Dad!

Brothers, this is a very special and powerful time with him. I let Dad take the lead and talk about what he wants to talk about, when he feels like talking. Before the symptoms accelerate is our opportunity for quality time with him.

That's it for now. The brief time I was back home between visits here, I felt closer to Dad than ever, as though he was in the next room. I imagine this will again be the case once I leave.

Let's stay in close touch. You are all such remarkable people. It's an honor to be your sister.

With love,

Fave Sis

Tuesday

Dearest Brothers,

Glad to arrive home yesterday for a short time and happy to hear things are going so well with Dad.

Tuesday: CONFIRMED: Victor for Dad's Beckwitz/IV appt. and shopping at Ralphs for groceries.

Wednesday: CONFIRMED: Victor is taking Dad to Ralphs (their new coupons come out today, he's very excited about that), and then Moshe is taking Dad to lunch.

Thursday: CONFIRMED: Dad's pinochle game, one of the players will drive him there and back.

Friday: CONFIRMED: Jackie's taking Dad to lunch, probably at Stanley's, and then dropping him off for an overnight stay at Tommy's for Shabbat dinner.

Saturday: CONFIRMED: Tommy is driving Dad home.

Sunday: Moshe and/or family will visit, since it's worked well the past couple weeks?

Monday: Phil, ditto?

Tuesday: CONFIRMED: Victor for Dad's Beckwitz/ IV apt. and shopping as needed. (Also, this is the day that Jackie Sunshine returns from Canada and she may want to see Dad in the evening. He'll probably let us know, is my guess, or anyone wanting to go over might enquire about their plans.)

Wednesday: (Guys, here you see we can repeat the schedule, squeezing brother Jackie in somewhere—though I know you're really, really busy, Jackie. Let me know!)

Love as always,

F.S.

Getting the Plants In for Winter

"**D**eath like birth is something we cannot control."
Sharon's empowering voice sheds light on my unspoken questions. "Your father's due date is out there in the ether and we don't know when that will be. Just trust it's all perfect and that God has a plan. Your dad is getting some quality time with everyone. It's hard. I experienced it with my mom, and she was around a lot longer.

"Lila, my feeling from you is that you think if you get this all figured out, then it won't hurt. You *have* to grieve. It's *going* to hurt. This pain is your grief and working on it is exactly what you need to be doing. The pain doesn't mean you're not 'getting it' spiritually. You know, we put so many conditions on ourselves as people on a spiritual path. It doesn't do any good to pretend you're not who you are. Feel what you're feeling without any judgment. Your feelings are genuine and it's okay to feel them. You need to grieve. If not, there will be problems. The more you process and cry and feel, the better off you'll be when your dad is gone. This is simply your way of preparing and working through it.

"It's perfect for both of you when you're there with your dad. This is quality time that you're giving to him and sharing together. No time is perfect on this planet. In between your father's angry jabs are some very dear times with him. Trust me—when you look back, you'll see this summer as quality time with him. *Lila dear, you're in a grieving process.* Sometimes you feel you're on top of it, and sometimes not. You're just working through it and so the sadness is perfect. Don't equate 'sad' with 'worse.' This *is* the work! You're working on releasing your dad, and it's painful and hard. You can't get around it.

"I think it's especially hard watching men die. Women seem to pass more graciously. Men struggle because their identity is all about being strong and independent.

"It's good your father still has time alone to work on his own issues, even though he may not be aware consciously of what he's doing. Whatever this time means to him, it's easier for him to do his inner work when he's alone."

Guys/Gal:

Myron took Dad to Stanley's today for lunch, and I joined them. Dad looked real good. His coloring was good and his energy was strong as well. He ate a healthy lunch, and we had a fine time.

Two days ago, Noah asked me if I was allergic to anything. I told him, "Dust. It makes me sneeze."

I asked him if he was allergic to anything and he said,

"No, I'm not allergic to anything, I just have allergies."
Talk to you all later.
Love,
Tommy

"It's not unusual for your father to want to drive," Sharon counsels me. "He needs to understand that he's putting others, not just himself, at risk. It's quite common for older people to have to stop driving since their reflexes are no longer sharp. The chemo is a form of life support and it's extending his life. When he's told to stop driving, a family member should be there as well as the doctor.

"Lila, it sounds like you see more than he's aware of feeling. Staying in denial even until he dies may be a part of his coping mechanism. I used to feel strongly that people have a right to know what's going on for them, yet some people don't want to know. This is not dementia on their part, though it may be an error in judgment. The steroids make your dad feel high like he can do anything. They can give him a false sense of his abilities even when he's off them.

"Now, here's something about the grieving process, in reference to Elizabeth Kubler-Ross' work with the five stages of grief: you don't just pass through the steps and then you're finished. You cycle through them every time a new issue surfaces like not driving or discovering there's a low blood count. Studies show these steps: denial, anger, bargaining, acceptance, and depression. As things change for him, you may see your father moving in and out of these stages. Maybe it's a blessing that you stay with him in shorter visits for the time being. The chemo can only do so much. At some point he'll shift and then leave quickly.

"Stay in that space of today. *Just take one day at a time.*"

With this geographic break from my father, I sense our connection is now beyond time and space. Always he is with me.

As I'm driving home from my office at Ananda Village after completing some quiet catch-up projects, what appears to be a largish stone in the middle of the road begins to move. *Very slowly.* The tortoise makes his way onto the blacktop road from nearby Turtle Pond. I bring my car to a stop on the gravel shoulder and coax him onto my clipboard to return him to the water's edge. He looks up at me, turns away, and not once but twice from instinctive fear urinates on my notepapers. My act of heroism may have cost me the notepad, but it probably saved his life.

My own life seems to have slowed to a tortoise-crawl. The cadence of time has become a clock with a run-down battery. What's more, the quality of my life has changed. With Dad's imminent passing, it feels as though my heart has been pummeled open, revealing lessons everywhere I turn, including my dome-shelled reptilian friend. The little fellow seems somehow symbolic of the continuity of existence: that life plods along before we die and will do so once we're gone. *Your father's due date is out there in the ether and we don't know when that will be. Just trust that it's all perfect and that God has a plan.*

Sometime later, I stumble upon Stanza 2:58 of the Indian scriptural classic, *The Bhagavad Gita*: "When the yogi, like a tortoise withdrawing its head and limbs into its shell, is able to withdraw his energy from the objects of sense-perceptions, he becomes established in wisdom."[4]

My silent prayer for my father is that he may enjoy his games and treasures in this world with inner freedom.

"I just wanted to say hi, Dad." My phone displays in crisp numbers the duration of our talk as three minutes long.

"You're very kind. You take care."

That's it?

Yes, that's it. That's all he has to say. Just checking in with my father while he's still here to check in with.

This time with Dad is so dear yet so uncomfortable. Although much is transpiring in my heart and mind, I've let these past few weeks go undocumented. My soul feels stretched beyond its natural ability to endure such trials. The echoes of last Tuesday's chemotherapy and steroids pulse through the slower tone of Dad's voice, faulty memory, slurred speech. Today he sounds better.

His outer life continues as usual—shopping for food at his favorite grocery stores, enjoying meals out and at home, visiting with family, playing cards and Scrabble, and watching television, though sparsely. Aaron has never been an avid fan of the telly. Why waste valuable time? Yet a good Clint Eastwood or Jimmy Stewart film never fails to find him settled on the sofa, remote control in hand.

"You know, Linda," Dad says on the phone, "my family never celebrated birthdays until your ma came into the family."

"Is that so?"

"September of 1949 was the year I had my first birthday party. Ever."

"Wow, that's ree-ally something! Any other news?"

"Today I played Scrabble with Jackson." Dad sounds more alert than yesterday. Nothing like a good board game to quicken the life force. "Linnie, I scored nearly four hundred points! I went out with all my letters on the word 'infarcts.'"

"Im-*pressive!*"

"Boy oh boy, was I ever lucky to find such a good Scrabble player—someone who can keep score too!"

"Being a guy means your dad probably doesn't want to talk about anything that's deep inside of him. It's just the way men are." This voicemail from my friend Prakash whose mother passed recently rallies my spirits. "We find that we're weakened by talking about our innermost feelings whereas women seem to get stronger from it. I know I never felt guided to get my mom to talk about these things. It wasn't her nature. Her life's mission was to be a lady. It just wouldn't have been the right way to do things. She would simply ask for the strength she needed. That's what comes to me to share with you. I don't know if this helps.

"Use your strength that you've developed over the years, Lila, to send the thought very strongly to your dad's soul that there's nothing to fear, because of *course* he has the strength and courage to deal with whatever comes. He's done it many times before. It seems funny to say, but he's always survived, probably a million times like the rest of us. You know and I know he's going to make it. It's just the transition that's a little spooky. My operating principle is something I learned from our friend Durga when Paula was in the hospital. I went to see her and didn't know what to do. So I was hanging around being the grandma as usual. Then Paula called me in to talk to her. I must have looked odd because Durga shrugged her shoulders and said, 'It's her party.'

"That's the right way to look at it. It's your dad's party, and you're just there to be in a supportive role so he can wrap up his business. Just be available for him.

"When my mother passed, the hospice people were absolutely wonderful. They have a little booklet called *Gone from My Sight*. Hospice is not a death sentence. It's a fine support system. Those are the best of the best, their nurses and health professionals. They're just excellent. We didn't even tell Mom at first that's who they were but she knew what was going on. You can call them and say, 'I think we're in a decline and I'd like to consider having my loved one in the program.'"

"Once only did your Uncle Mickey and I talk about his military experience," Dad says over the phone. "Mick started to cry. He'd won a bronze star in the war. I learned of it for the first time only recently. They got a replacement of his medal for bravery, a bronze star. I never knew he had it since 1945. We're talking sixty-three years of secrecy." Dad continues more slowly. "It was a great hardship for him. Both his legs got frozen. That's how bad the conditions were. Your uncle gets disability from being in the service, they send him a check every month.

"Mick just turned eighty-five years old. He's taking it one day at a time."

"I like what you said in your voicemail about your dad," Prakash says in his follow-up phone message. "I think you're tuning in very well.

"My own dad died of heart failure. He got quite weak at the end, but he still insisted on keeping his routine. Toward the end he actually pushed himself upstairs to his office on his hands and knees, taking care of business as usual. He was 'getting the plants in for winter.' On my last visit when he could barely stand, he cooked a meal for the family. Obviously that's what he wanted to do. He was the father providing for his family, and I think that's where his strength and his ability to deal with what happened came from. We all honored it. I don't think we thought about it or talked about it. It was just an understanding of what he needed to do in his dying process.

"I think you're right. Just honor your dad's way of being and let him know that you receive it—that you receive his protection and his fatherly care and that you are nourished and benefited by his strength. And that reinforces him and provides an environment in which he can find a deeper strength to accept the transition that's coming. That generation too that they call the greatest generation, the World War II generation—the fathers were *patres familias* and the moms made a home. It was a different era. To some extent, it's archetypal and partly it's cultural and historical to that time period.

"Yet I think there's a lot of eternal truth in those roles and ways of being."

Five minutes to the second is the length of today's phone visit. Dad sounds very positive, strong. He endured well his second chemotherapy treatment this morning, and Dr. Beckwitz says he likes the way my father looks.

How is it that whenever I call, he makes a point of telling me he's in the middle of a huge meal with the appetite of a triathlete? This time it's a Saunders hot fudge sundae with a topping so buttery I can almost taste it through the mouthpiece. *Should I believe him or is he fabricating this comfort food?* And is it for his comfort—or mine?

"Linnie, listen to me." My parent's voice streams forcefully through the phone line. "I'm looking forward to seeing you next week."

This business-as-usual attitude is Dad dealing with his imminent departure from this world. Directing our discussion to the point of choking it, he controls its length, its content, says what he wants to say, and ends abruptly with, "I love you." That's all. No wasting of words, least of all on the phone.

You know he's going to make it. It's just the transition that's a little spooky.

"Guess what, Dolly? I played checkers with Noah today," Dad tells me in our next phone conversation. "I let him jump me."

"You *what*? You let him *jump* you?"

In vividly rendered colors, I recall being five years old and playing checkers with my father. I would face him squarely across the board, trying willfully to make my presence bigger. My skinny little legs hung like half-cooked spaghetti noodles below the chair seat while my feet dangled in mid-air, too short for my sneakers to scrape the floor.

Never once did my father let me win. No matter how hard I tried, I could never manage to beat him.

Dad didn't play easy with me. His focus was fierce and his

concentration was unbroken, if not legendary. My ill-fated checker pieces were doomed to be cornered, trapped, and eventually eliminated from the glass board of sixty-four red and black squares. His bold double-stacked kings chased my pieces, flimsy and quivering, that scuttled from one corner of the board to the other— diagonally, backwards, forwards like the ambivalent torrents of heavy rain in the Umbrian hills where I would one day live. I watched with trepidation until piece by piece I was hopelessly jumped and eventually terminated. Fuming with frustration I plotted my next move, again to find myself double- or triple-jumped. With only five years of life experience to draw on, I was not yet a deft strategist. Defeat never rang true to my father's nature, nor to mine. Yet despite my repeated efforts, my best was never quite good enough. How could I not feel overpowered, overwhelmed, completely out of my league when matching wits with my father?

"*Nu*, Dad, so what's the deal? *You let Noah jump you?* Please tell me you're joking. Why didn't you ever let *me* win?"

"It was to make you tough, Linnie."

"Well, then. It worked. You made me tough." *So tough that I was able to forge the strength to live my own life. And to help you complete yours.* How did my father know that letting Noah win would strengthen him and yet weaken me?

Dad is right whether I like it or not. He exemplifies the words of my Guru—though he'll never hear this from *my* lips: "We don't get strong by wrestling with weaklings."

Father mine, as would be translated from the poetic Hebrew: My gladness is both deep and still that your last days are filled with joy.

My Mother's Crayons

"**M**ommy, will you color with me?" I asked.

"Not now, my love, I'm sweeping the floor."

"Aft-e-e-r?"By elongating a word in my mouth to twice its actual syllables, I found I could stretch it like saltwater taffy. Especially when I whined. Words were so much fun to play with!

"After." She replied with the patience and charity of unconditional love.

The scratchings of scattered corn flakes and dried macaroni noodles, like the words that rattled in my mouth, caught in the bristles of Harriet's broom across the kitchen floor. Mother and daughter sat together. The one in her mid-twenties, the other barely six years old. I perched in Mom's lap and flipped through my favorite coloring book on a quest to find the perfect line drawings for our art work. My petal pusher pants exposed the tomboy dirt around my ankles, testimony to my fierce aversion to bathtubs. Much like a crocheted quilt of pure, creative inspiration, the aura of my mother's love settled on our home. *No one colors quite like her—no one. How does she do it?* Her artistry left me baffled, awestruck. The crayons danced in her deft hands, splashing life force across the coarse pages of my book.

To make our coloring sessions intellectually challenging and creatively expansive to my insatiable mind, I invented a guessing game all about intuiting my mother's choice of colors. Her decisions infinitely surprised me. *Which crayon will she choose next?* A bold teal for the king's hunting outfit. A burnt red for the door of the gnome's cave. *Ree-ally?* So many questions spun round my head. *Why, why, why?* Always my guesses were uncannily, consistently wrong. The figures touched by her crayons turned to figurines. They sighed and spoke beneath her fingers. *And they like to play with their words too!* I curled up in her lap like a braided Sabbath *challah* and watched my tiny universe expand as each new character became a best friend. The dragon's hot breath singed the thin skin of the aristocrat who then gave the beast a verbal slashing. The swish of the princess's silken dress caught on the low tree branches and whooshed in her ears as she uttered her dismay to the green perennials. How wonderfully Mom shaded the skirt of the royal girl standing before the twisted trunk of the oak tree!

With what abandon she colored. Mom rendered a subtlety on the pages to which I could only aspire. And she always stayed within the lines. *How* did *she do it?*

Watching my mother's deft artistry generated frustration within my immature sense of coordination. Held between my unwieldy fingers, the crayons snapped crisply in half. Sometimes it was more fun to press the sticks of colored wax into the paper as hard as I could just to get something, anything, onto the page. What I lacked in grace I compensated for in brute strength.

Maybe someday I too will own the patience to hold a crayon lightly like a feather, shading from the outer edges to the center ever so softly. Just like my mother.

Harriet had the delicate hands of a princess. Her slender fingers with their pink tapered nails looked as though they'd never even held a broom let alone done any sort of menial work. Some years back, they seemed to flutter like feathers in the wind, lightly touching down on the covers of her hospital bed as she lay in a coma just before passing from this world to the next.

Mom died seven years before Dad. A surgery resulting in complications rendered her comatose with no clinically detectable brain activity. The operation left an incision along the side of her torso not unlike a sorry roadmap. Yet those last two weeks of her life may have been the most important, to her and to her family. Dad, the brothers, and me rallied night and day around her bedside. As with baby Shmuel hospitalized after his birth, we saw to it that she was never without family.

A stream of raucous laughter overestimating the boundaries of its banks rang from her hospital room and down the sterile hall to the nursing station. Moshe, oh, he got upset with our lack of decorum! He even stormed out the door a time or two. Such behavior might be admissible at a loved one's *shiva*, but not in the more somber moments around a dying parent. Yet we couldn't help ourselves. The joy of family bonds sought release through our joviality.

Mom was back. Her soul hovered above her deathbed, much like the swimming goddess of yore, diving through the waves of illusory time and leaving not a single ripple.

No brain activity? *Or simply that the diagnostic machines were not sophisticated enough to measure the pulse of the human spirit?* Whenever my father walked into the room, Mom sent him tiny kisses through her oxygen mask, her eyes shining with recognition. "Ya had ta see it," Moshe said. For those two weeks—including being taken off life support for eight days and rallying a few days longer once it was restored—Mom was more our mother than she'd been for decades. She was the life of the party, one held in her honor.

I had never lost a mother before, at least not in this lifetime. Late at night, considering the nine-hour time difference from Los Angeles to Italy, I rang my friend and guide, Swami. His first words to me were, "Liladevi, what are you doing up so late?" He then offered suggestions to help me bear the imminent loss that shadowed my heart.

Such was the closeness between mother and daughter that Mom could not leave this world until I'd left Los Angeles. I flew home on a Friday. The next morning, a fitful nap in my own bed carried me from one dreamlike state to another like flipping through the pages of my coloring book. *What colors will Mom choose next?* I awoke half an hour later with the knowing that she had gone.

"Didn't you hear?" a soft-spoken nurse asked when I phoned the hospital. "Your mother just passed."

Death, like birth, is something we cannot control. Families want to be at the bedside, yet it's often when they leave that the person passes.

The bigger picture is that we can plan or tamper all we want but when it's time to go, it's time to go.

A mother's love is an ethereally transcendent expression of the Divine. As unwell as she remained throughout most of her adult life, Harriet loved her children dearly. That love was ever-present even through the many chasms of illness into which she sank over the years to the despair of her family. Although such difficulties diminished her greatly, they never touched her ability to love. She held within her essence, like her drawings that always stayed within the lines, so many pieces of my present incarnation. I always enjoyed hearing her accounts of my early life—not so much out of vanity as to help me understand myself more deeply.

"When you were only two years old, Linda, you were already asking about God," Mom told me many years later. "You wanted to know, 'Who is God?' 'Who made the clouds?' 'Who made God?'"

Even then, big questions filled my soul that would one day be answered to my full satisfaction by my chosen spiritual path. At a very young age I was to discover a spark of Christianity within my own home—a far cry from orthodox though Jewish nonetheless. A Renaissance art book belonging to Harriet unlocked great treasures for her little daughter. The artistic renderings left me transfixed. Fra Angelico, a monk and a painter, portrayed *The Annunciation* with a mixture of reality and holiness. Leonardo da Vinci's poetic brush captured the beatific consciousness of the young Mary while an angel pointed toward the sacred baby and the blessed child John in *Madonna of the Rocks. The Supper at Emmaus* by Rembrandt depicted a radiant light around the Christ filled with divinity and humanity, blessing both the bread and the disciples before vanishing from their physical sight.

Harriet was deluged with my tireless questions. "Mama, who is this baby with this woman?" And, "Who is this man, and why is he nailed to the wood with his arms sticking out like that?"

"Oh, he's no one special. He's just a man—not even a prophet, really. Just a man."

Her explanations mattered little to me. My full enrapt attention was upon him. As I would learn many years later, Christ is a consciousness in human form: of expansion inclusive of all living things; of forgiveness beyond self-limiting egoism; of love greater than mere law. "Christ was crucified once," my Guru explained. "But his teachings have been crucified every day for two thousand years." My mother's art book conveyed to my mind the universality of truth through its timeless and classic paintings. It exemplified as I was to learn many years later that: "Truth is one and eternal. Realize oneness with it in your deathless Self, within." [5]

THAT SCRABBLE GAME IN THE SKY

I arrive back in Los Angeles greeted by a very hot day—hot in the way that Los Angeles heats up—and blanketed in a film of grimy pollution that makes you not want to breathe too deeply for fear of inhaling airborne impurities. Your cells want the oxygen but not the baggage that comes with it. I feel a great passion of creative intensity and love for my spiritual path in this moment between the fractured pieces of my struggling heart. I want to breathe. I want to create. I want to live. Somewhere in a spiritual community north of the madness of this ecstatic city, my kitties snore in their sleep, napping on a sofa in my other life, whenever they please and without a care in their furry heads as their soft paws curl around their faces like smoke rings in the crushing heat.

Sad thoughts shuttle through my mind at the Burbank Airport. The luggage belt coughs out my suitcase.

Dad isn't here to greet me.

Always his smile precedes him: the smile of the young Aaron selling cold sodas on hot Chicago summer days; of Zeke in his naval uniform daring life to test its luck with him; of my father looming bigger than life in my forever-child memory.

Dad's not here, and my insides are hollow. Ironically in some ways, he's never been there for me. In other ways, he's never *not* been there—prompt, dependable, sharply dressed—ready to take my luggage and take care of his little girl. His gait would be definitive and steady. His shoes would click crisply on the baked pavement, each step landing precisely where he commands it to.

I *schlep* my unwieldy suitcase, carry-on bag, and heavy purse across the chaotic street to take my place like a piece on a checker board in the queue for a cab.

Aaron waits outside his condominium building, tucked safely under the entrance canopy out of reach from the harsh sun. The life-sustaining star is now adversarial to his chemotherapy-drenched skin.

My taxi arrives.

Dad pays the driver without adding a tip. The steroids preceding the previous day's treatment seem to trigger strong personality changes, making him more aggressive and less himself. A terrible row ensues with the silver-haired Russian cab driver. *Is Dad angry that he can't take care of his daughter? That the driver, a stranger, has to do it for him?*

Retreating into the shade of the canopy, I witness the enactment of the surreal drama while pondering the nature of reality like an actor in a play who forgets his lines, derails from the script, and begins to adlib."Who *are* you," I want to ask Dad, "and what have you done with my father?" The dreamlike scene passes before my eyes:

Life is a dream, time like a stream
Carries our burdens away.
Never despair, joy's everywhere,
Love can befriend you today.[6]

"That guy wanted *wa-ay* too big of a tip," Dad says in a huff, "and I'm not going to be taken advantage of. Oh, *no-o*. What does he think I am, made of money?"

My father is wearing a stained tee-shirt with a frayed collar that has long since turned to rags. His faded blue jeans are nearly threadbare at the knees. They too are stained. He has shrunk down exactly two sizes, from a forty to a thirty-six waist. The smaller garments fit him perfectly.

"Don't fuss with my clothes, Linda. Just leave them be."

The spool of thread, measuring tape, sewing needle, and the tin of straight pins that I packed to hem his trousers—now hanging loosely to the floor—will remain tucked away in my suitcase. Aaron's pride dictates that he wants no attention paid to his waning size. Clearly the weight loss distresses him.

Dad looks like a different person with a new strained expression on his face. His energy is withdrawn. He's less outward, no longer interested in interacting with the storyline in the world around him. These changes alarm and sadden me. Life may indeed be a dream, but I'm not ready to see the dream of my father's life come to an end. Not now. Not yet. *Is anyone ever ready to say good-bye to a loved one?*

Introspection born of the inner sight of a spiritual life and meditating daily for decades grants me the realization that my pain stems from two attitudes, both understandable though neither of them helpful! One is a focus on myself—*my* loss and *my* life without *my* father. The focus here is on . . . my own self. The other attitude is one of resistance toward what's happening and a desire that circumstances be other than they are. *This is all exactly right. Everything Dad's telling us is true.* It's time for him to move on and for us to continue without him. My father is on his way to Heaven.

"Dad, did I ever tell you about my friend who passed away from a similar kind of cancer?" He plies me with questions about Carolyn's final weeks, reclining in bed with an authoritative air and seeking a comfort that my answers cannot seem to give him.

"Did she get brain cancer, too?"

"No, she didn't. You know, it doesn't spread to the brain for everyone." What most frightens him is the thought of this disease robbing him of his mental faculties.

I am much relieved that it's easier than I'd anticipated to see Dad after being gone for a few weeks. I'm happy to be back. Thinner by about ten pounds, he now wears that deep low "cancer brow" that Carolyn developed shortly before she died. His forehead is frozen in gaunt, furrowed rows, perhaps from asking inwardly without ceasing, "Why, God? *Why did this happen to me?*"

Our first day together is full and immensely tiring for Dad. Even so, his strength of will astounds me. To celebrate my return, we go out to lunch and then to dinner with Jackson. I find all the hubbub a little exhausting, especially on the same day with a long drive to the airport and a short flight back to Los Angeles. I cannot tell if my father wants to show me that he's well and energetic or if the IV steroids are driving him in unnatural ways. Or if he's trying to squeeze every possible drop from life to share with his only daughter.

At the fancy restaurants with their bouncy music and crisp table cloths, Dad eats little but well, seeming to greatly enjoy his food. *Is this an act for my benefit?* True to the nature of an accomplished storyteller, he shows rather than tells me how he's doing. We return home to play cards, each winning a game. The phone rings, heralding a call from my-brother-the-doctor whose voice exudes the bold-scented confidence he inherited from his father.

"Hiya, Sis! Glad to have ya back, how's it going?"

"Oh, pretty super, I guess. Tell me, Phil, how'd you do at last night's poker game?"

"Let me put it this way—I made a nice contribution to the game."

"So-o, you lost?"

"That's one way to look at it. Dad there?" I pass the phone to our parent who shuffles a deck of cards between nibbles of a soft-baked packaged cookie.

"I can understand why Grampa Levine's second marriage to Lillian Finck didn't work," Dad tells Phil. "Older people have trouble changing their ways."

Dad seems distraught today like a card deck not thoroughly shuffled. A misplaced check for three thousand dollars has unsettled him. "I swear, Dolly, when it arrived last Monday, I set it on my desk. Somebody stole that check. I'm *sure* of it," he says, both hesitant and certain. Messy as the desktop is, it's a wonder more papers aren't lost! *Father mine, be at peace. It's doubtful that anyone has broken in to steal anything. . .*

"Linnie, are you meditating?" Dad's request trails from his bedroom a little earlier than usual.

"Almost done, what's on your mind?"

As I lunge forward, my foot catches clumsily on the foldout sofa's mismatched synthetic sheets whose plum and peach colors add little to the décor of the cluttered guest room. This is The Lumpiest Bed Ever. Laying on it is like napping on a plate of spaghetti with meatballs.

My meditation beads slip from my hands. The necklace of *rudraksha* seeds strung together with a coarse thread land on the carpet with a light, woody thump. I love the touch of them, each bead a tiny prayer that echoes in the cave of my meditations.

"Linda, I want to tell you a story." My father's voice ricochets through the hallway, tittering with the gleeful anticipation of a child about to tattle on his friend.

"Be right there, I can finish meditating later."

Dad proceeds to tell me about how, after his brother Joe left their home in the slums of Chicago, the remaining six family members shared a tiny apartment with one bathroom. Often someone had to go "make" in the back alley where garbage was freely thrown.

"That's why I've always enjoyed material pleasures so much," Dad says lightly. The joy in his eyes punctuates the ending of his story. "To have risen out of such poverty is quite an accomplishment for me. Sister, let's call Sue."

Our friend in Michigan is nearing her sixty-sixth birthday. Dad's a chipper conversationalist on the telephone.

"Hey there, Susie. It's me, Zeke. I'm getting ready to go to that big Scrabble game in the sky."

EPICENTER OF A WOK

Tofu is an acquired taste, one that many people fail to acquire in their lifetime.

One might argue that it *has* no taste and no identity of its own, instead stealing flavors from other ingredients in the wok. Few and far between are the eateries that do it justice. Even restaurants that cater exclusively to a vegetarian palate often find the curdled soybean milk an oddity. Spices cannot embellish it; overcooking does not enhance it. Formless, flavorless, and genetically modified if not organic, bean curd is an absurdity bordering on an anomaly to most main courses, even when the chef conjures his best magic to doctor it beyond recognition. Tofu, in point of fact, lacks culinary integrity. Most restauranteurs might think when contemplating adding it to their menu, *why bother?* Rarely if ever will true carnivores of their own volition order a dish with tofu as an ingredient. *What are they, nuts?*

That's why Dad loves treating me to lunch at Bamboo on Ventura Boulevard. Their sweet and sour tofu is beyond reproach.

Only the best for his little girl. Bamboo with its valet parking may be the only Asian restaurant that—instead of Chinese rock music with its distinctive nasal twang potentially disruptive to the digestion of some patrons—pipes in Italian opera, creating a perfect ambiance for enjoying egg rolls.

Yet to one little princess, lunch is not about the music. Or the mu shui. Or The World's Best Tofu.

It's about being with her father.

Yesterday's Chinese lunch causes Dad to suffer acute abdominal pain. Severe cramping keeps him bedridden throughout the early morning. No more egg rolls. No more wanton crackers. Fried food is now on the "no" list for his compromised digestive system. If his diet were up to me—which it's not, nor should it be—the richer deeply fried, heavily processed foods would have been discontinued long ago.

This is your father's party. You're just there to host it.

"Now the symptoms are starting." My father gazes from his pillow into the ether. "My heart will probably give out first." Little did we know then how prophetic his words would be.

"How does that feel to you, Dad?"

"Darlin'," he replies in a mock Irish accent with a leprechaun twinkle in his eyes, "me time is runnin' out."

At Dr. Beckwitz's office the next day, Dad relays to the oncologist a progress report on his condition. The Tarceva is now sapping him instead of zapping him. His failing body is overwhelmed. The mercurially quick-minded doctor swivels on his stool-on-wheels, scooting himself across the room to the treatment table where my father sits.

"Zeke," he says, thoughtful and deliberate, breaking an interminably long silence. "I'm going to make an executive decision here. Let's take you off the Tarceva."

"*What?*" Dad snaps, exhaling as if the breath in his lungs has been forcibly removed. "Are you trying to *kill* me?" His eyes flash with an anger that is perhaps too well controlled. The drug, still considered experimental in many medical circles, is a potentially life-lengthening medication albeit with a list of horrific side effects. Having it discontinued Dad interprets as a death sentence. The doctor-patient dialogue lingers in the room, its walls unable to assimilate what they've just been privy to hear.

Life is a dream.

"We'll keep you on the chemo IV treatments, Zeke. Hopefully, they'll slow things down," Dr. Beckwitz says, already halfway out the door.

Following the swish of her starched white uniform more formal than the gown of the princess my mother once colored, a Hispanic nurse taps on the door. Like a swan on the surface of a pond, she glides into the room in her square-soled nursing shoes.

Time like a stream carries our burdens away. She draws Dad's blood and preps his vein with a stint. Escorting my father down the endless hallway to the IV room, the nurse exudes the grace of a hostess at a fine restaurant ushering a patron to his table with her please-follow-me gait, where a surreptitiously-given tip will ensure a choice booth with a stunning view.

The nursing station swarms with staff. The long room looks even longer with a dozen IV patients seated in a dozen cushioned recliner chairs. A bookcase with pillows and blankets lines the far wall. People of all ages and cultures sit hooked up to the intravenous drugs. Some have nodded off to pass the time, slumped over in their sweaters and blankets. All look disheartened, despairing, weary.

Except my father.

"So tell me, Sandra," Dad says to the nurse assembling his IV, "how's your Scrabble game these days?

"Joanne, are you married? If the answer's yes, do you happen to have any pictures of your children with you?

"Say, Janine, I bet you play a mean game of Texas hold 'em!"

The room brightens with Dad in it. The walls appear freshly painted, the floor newly waxed. In Aaron's presence, everyone seems to perk up. He chats matter-of-factly with the nurses, comporting himself more like a gentleman on a sales call than a patient about to receive chemotherapy. My father sprinkles the room with life force. Living in this world without him is something I cannot imagine.

Never despair, joy's everywhere. Love can befriend you today.

A modern-day town crier, the squat outdated television set in the waiting room blares the day's national news. There I sit silent and alone, a five-year-old waiting to play checkers with her dad. I thumb absent-mindedly through a hodge-podge of tattered magazines, wondering how many sad, frightened, and hopeful relatives of cancer patients have left their unseen fingerprints on the frayed pages. And how many of them have drawn courage from their spiritual beliefs to rejoice in their loved one's imminent transition to the astral world.

Of a sudden without warning, the walls start to move. First to the left, then to the right.

Ohmygawd, what's this?

Squared angles morph into sextiles before my eyes. I am at sea in an epicenter of chaos. The scene grows even more surreal with everybody tending to business as usual. *As if nothing uncommon is happening!*

Earthquakes in Los Angeles are presumed commonplace, this one a 5.8 on the Richter Scale. Its epicenter froths and gurgles in the underground of Chino Hills. Fortunately no lives are lost, though many structures sustain damage and nearby amusement parks close their rides.

The tremors leave me visibly shaken. My father, not at all.

"See how scared my daughter is?" Dad appoints himself the town crier of the chemotherapy ward. His disproportionately large grin announces my distress to the nurses. Is this his way of affirming he's braver than me? In command of the situation? Still in control of the crumbling domain of his body?

Truth is, Dad, this earthquake pales in comparison to what I'm inwardly enduring with your imminent passing.

THE CHEMO TWO-STEP

The birth of a butterfly is a perfect metaphor for the struggles we must endure in this world in order to grow spiritually. The insect's efforts to break free of her hard-shelled chrysalis-womb pump the blood and life force into her wings that give her the ability to get on with living. Her strength to fly is both hard won and necessary for her survival.

You might say she hits the ground running.

I often feel like a butterfly, energetically speaking, especially these days. Today isn't the happiest of birthdays for me, but at least it's spent with my father. Cousin Bevvie phones, and she and Dad chat lightly. "Your dad always makes *me* feel good whenever I call," she tells me afterwards. "He lights up when I visit. What a special person he is."

Our customary corner of the back patio of Stanley's Restaurant on Ventura Boulevard awaits my birthday lunch. Dad, Jackson, Jackie, and I take our seats in the airy spot, sunlit and somewhat private. A round of water glasses with slices of lemon prefaces our meal. "No ice for me," I tell the waiter. "I'm not an ice person," which always sounds like saying, "I'm not a nice person."

Dad hands me a birthday card illustrated with water-color butterflies before the timely arrival of appetizers. I'd like to think he knows about my resonance with the *Lepidoptera* order. The sentimental Hallmark message with its borders hazed between understatement and *schmaltz* could have been written by him. In those magical ways that Spirit like a butterfly lands on the indelible moments of our lives, a woman at a nearby table offers to take our picture, immortalizing that moment in time for my birthdays to come when Dad won't be around to give me a *schmaltzy* greeting card.

Click.

My last birthday with my father.

Once home, the parent delivers a most enticing sales pitch. He convinces me to call my brothers one by one, pleading his case to be allowed to drive again. "Not on the freeways, Linnie," he says reassuring no one, "just around the neighborhood." Desperation fuels his struggle to maintain some remnant of the independence that "the disease" is wrestling from his grip. Yet despite his best efforts, we five offspring are not impressed.

The brothers cast their votes. No one is comfortable with him driving. And yet—Dad is Dad. Our provider, protector, and care-giver has thoroughly hypnotized the lot of us.

It's brother Jackie who remains adamant. "To let Dad continue driving is unacceptable. I won't stand for it."

Our middle sibling addresses the anxiety that flits like butterflies in the pit of our awareness. We all want to accommodate Dad; yet no one wants him driving. Of *course* it's the right decision, as everyone knows. But that doesn't make it any easier.

Even so, something tells me this is a sham. I suspect Dad will jolly well drive for as long as he is able and whenever he pleases. We all see the part of Dad that's doing not just fine but great. Surely strong people draw strong tests. On a soul level, I know my father is untouched by the harsh symptoms that are vacating him from his body. Most importantly, he seems to be receiving our love.

My father's birthday card—I will keep it always.

The clock strikes midnight, burying its face on a shelf in the linen closet. It whimpers into a pile of folded washcloths precisely where I hid it, and where it belongs. With its soulless conglomeration of battery-operated plastic and metallic parts, its incessant time-keeping disrupts my thinning sanity, reminding me that my father's life is ticking away, and calling to mind Swami's admonishing words: "I always tell people not to get old, but nobody listens!"

The faint clicking is drowned out by my crying in the foldout bed in the guest room. The irregular-sized sheets bought on sale decades earlier fit the mattress poorly, and the down comforter reeks with a dank odor of mildew. *This sofa is a joke. Sleeping on it is pure austerity.* The hinges of the metal frame squeal whenever I move as though the bed considers me an unwieldy burden that might simply disappear.

I hate crying. But even more so, stifling it. My heart is shattered into a million pieces and this is my worst birthday ever. Seeing Dad's nightstand light on as it often is in the late hours, I knock on the open door and step into his room.

"Stop crying," he says firmly. Which only makes me cry harder. "Stop that right now. I don't want to see you cry."

So small yet so feisty, my father leans lightly on his pillows. I fold my limbs on the corner of his bed like a washcloth in the linen closet. "Dad. I'm—very—upset." Never will I cease to amaze myself with my knack for stating the ridiculously obvious.

"Why, sweetie?" His knotted brow bunches up as if by exerting enough focused energy there, he might will away the burden of my sorrow.

Why am I upset? Ree-ally? Because you're dying! "I don't like the thought of your last days being spent with a paid caregiver instead of family. I won't have it."

"Linnie, your place is in your own home," Dad says in his listen-to-me-and-do-what-I-say tone. "I want you to be spared the suffering of seeing what's going to happen to me."

"Dad! Stop pushing me a-way." My vision dims with a fresh cycle of tears. I detest and welcome the flood, unwilling and unable to control it.

"I'm not pushing you away."

Seeing that I'm not about to back down, he seems to comprehend my decision—that I refuse to be denied the supreme honor of caring for my father. Finally this stubborn man relents. Tenderly he takes my hand. His arms appear thinner in his short-sleeved shirt, yet his grip is as vital as ever. Here lies a proud man, a patriarch and lord of his domain, alongside his eldest offspring—and a woman—telling him what to do. Though in the end, Dad seems resolute, even touched.

Oh, no-o, this isn't easy for him, not easy at all. Yet the next day when the emotional storm clouds have dispersed, he tells a Scrabble buddy on the telephone, "Sol, you remember my daughter?" His voice blares above a rowdy television Western. "She says she wants to take care of her ol' dad . . ."

Perhaps this is the best understanding we can reach, and it gives my heart peace. Maybe Dad's last story will tell itself better than he thinks. Maybe the hard part is over. *Please, God, let it be so.*

With an ache in my soul, I've wanted to have my father's wit in his own words, recorded digitally to share with our family in the years ahead. But he refuses. Of course, what was I thinking? Dad lives on his own terms and he'll die the same way. *Though it grieves me*, I dialogue to myself in the privacy of the guest room where I feel like anything but a guest, *I must let this go*. Like the Native Americans who distrust the technology of photography, believing that pictures trap their spirit, Aaron only tells his stories when and to whom he chooses.

Dad has been feeling like his old self again and is for the time being without pain. His thoughts are sharper and clearer. He's not quite as tired or irritable. Some quality of life seems to have returned, even though discontinuing the Tarceva marks a turning point for the cancer to spread more rapidly.

Alas, this symptom-free honeymoon is fated to be short-lived.

Aaron sets an unlit cigar on the cluttered coffee table. His bag of storytelling tricks never empties and even his oldest anecdotes are now embellished with new details. First in Dad's mental queue is his dancing partner Rochelle—who was according to him the best ever.

"Because I was so poor, we always went Dutch. I never got to meet her parents. For some reason they were always gone when I went to pick her up for a dance."

Dad shakes his head in disbelief at his own story, as if he himself has never heard it before and like his audience finds it completely incredulous. The years disappear. Once more I'm a little girl being tucked into bed by the sound of my father's voice, its lyrical melody blazing trails through my subconscious while sleep overtakes my spindly limbs and dark locks.

One of the nurses at Dr. Beckwitz's office, as it happens, is named Rochelle.

"Tell me, Rochelle, can you dance?"

Dad jumps off the examination table to take her lightly by the waist and lead her in a quick two-step across the floor of the prep room for chemotherapy patients.

How filled with contradictions is the human personality. Especially my father's. Dad decides to switch dry cleaners because the older location conveniently within walking distance just down the block is under new management. "They raised their prices, Linnie—by *twenty-five cents! Oygevalt*, shirts-schmirts. Now I have to take my business *and* my shirts elsewhere." *Yet he tells me I don't charge nearly enough for my courses and consultations?* "Time is money, Linda. That's what you don't understand." My father drives himself to excellence and as extensions of himself, his children as well. Many times he marvels at my mother's wisdom in choosing North Hollywood for their condominium. With only a short walk across the street for groceries and down the block for an excellent kosher restaurant—and formerly for his dry cleaning—he remembers Mom with great fondness.

"She ree-ally knew what she was doing, your mother," he says, switching channels with the remote control to check the day's stock prices.

"And could that gal ever cook."

BEEF STEW, WEDDED BLISS

Newlyweds Aaron and Harriet had nested in Chicago in the family home for barely a month. The bride's tears caused by being separated from her own family for the first time flowed freely and often. One evening before relocating back to Detroit, Harriet's dinner awaited her new spouse as he drove home from work. Brothers Frankie and Mickey preceded him.

They were first to taste the sorry cuisine.

"Beef stew? She doesn't really know what she's *doing*," Frankie whispered to Aaron in the narrow hallway. The floorboards creaked beneath their shoes, the wooden planks bowing with the weight of perhaps too much information.

"She thickened the gravy with great globs of white flour," Mickey said in a hushed breath. "It looks like paste and *tastes* like it too."

"We hate it." Frankie folded his arms with abrupt finality on the subject of dinner.

Mickey nodded as much in agreement as embarrassment. He looked toward the diffused light of the kitchen where a soft sobbing sound eked into the hallway. Aaron kissed away the salt tears and white flour streaked like melted cake frosting on his wife's cheeks. Dolefully and dutifully, she re-tied her apron strings before ladling a portion of the stew onto his plate.

The white glob sat listlessly on the white china.

An amorphous lump of a meal, it looked as though it too harbored embarrassment and wasn't quite sure what to do with itself.

"Mmmm," said Aaron, smacking his lips. And again, "Mmmm."

Dad shakes his head from side to side. "Then to make sure the compliment sank in," he tells me, reliving a memory as diffused as the hallway light of decades past, "I asked your ma for a second helping.

"You shoulda seen that gal smile."

She's Buying Me *Towels?*

I've gone home to the Sierra foothills and returned again. It's as though I never left nor will I ever leave my father.

Last night's poker game may have been Dad's last. All the guys saw him struggling. How Dad looks forward to his games: Thursday Scrabble with Konrad Schloss and his caregiver Noel just five minutes away; Friday afternoon pinochle also with Konrad and several other buddies of whom Dad enjoys being the youngest ("Norton's still driving, Linda, and he's ninety-one! *Nu*, can you believe it?"); and the weekly grand finale—the poker game on Friday night at the Mortesa mansion with the whole gang, including Phil, Jackie, and Tommy, plus Robert Katims and other special cronies. As I was never privileged to attend these sacred gatherings, I cannot comment further. Their poker night is a sacred ritual to the male gender and will forever remain so.

Dad's talk with Tommy by phone goes something like this: "Sonny, I've got something that's going to go on forever."

"What's that, Bupkes?" Tommy asks from his mobile while driving to his oceanside office.

"My family."

"Although Dad's a wounded soldier," Tommy tells me later, "he's enduring without complaint. Even though he's injured, he's still helping others. He did that for Mom and for cousin Peter, and now he's doing it for all of us."

"You got *that* right, Bro."

"Dad's very inspiring. It is what it is." Thus speaks my little brother in his big wisdom.

"At best, Zeke, this new chemotherapy medication might give you another two weeks," the oncologist explains. "It's more effective for breast and lung cancer. A few of the side effects are headaches, vomiting, and diarrhea."

"Oh? Then I decline it." Of all the decisions made by my father, perhaps none has been so poignant as the admission that his body has reached the limit of its ability to tolerate further invasive medicines. Yet he remains indomitable. I'm awed by what he has endured this far.

A holiday in Paris has Moshe's daughter Chana animated on the phone with her Zayde. They discuss the book of art through the ages that he'd entrusted to her without knowing it was the dearest treasure to me of all Mom's books. Learning this, my niece eagerly returned it to his care and thus to me. Its sentimental value cannot be measured, with the paintings of the baby and his mother and the man, "just a man," on the cross.

My Dear Brother Moshe,

How are you? It was lovely talking with you today.

I hope you're not in any way put off by Dad saying he didn't want to see you this afternoon. He was much more active today than he could handle. Jackie visited, then the hospice workers, then Tommy, Liz, and all the kids. Dad's sleeping now with a look of great exertion on his face. He said last night after everyone left:

"I can't handle visitors right now, I'm dying."

And yet as soon as he heard the door latch behind them, he watched two hours of baseball! Moshe, please know that the games relax him. As you know, I'm here in a different capacity than company—as a caregiver whose presence he's willing to accept.

What he told you on the phone this morning was very significant: "Stay close." It's in that context that he wants you here. Since I last saw Dad several weeks ago, his energy has declined. He knows his time is drawing near. In order to leave us, he needs to withdraw, especially from those he loves the most. I'm sharing this so you can know that you are most dear to him and that's precisely why he's withdrawing from you.

These are just some thoughts by way of updating you.

Thank you with all my heart that I may have this prized art book. It is rich with dearness to me.

Happy Sabbath with love,

Your Own Sister

The housekeeper cleans, dusts, washes, and scrubs for five hours.

"Mr. Zeke, you maybe sit in the living room rocker for an hour—not more, I promise you—while I clean your room?"

Too proud to admit the austerity of remaining upright that long is more than Dad can tolerate, he endures quietly and without complaint. The day is busy, too busy for his waning energy. Yet he rises to it. Moshe visits, followed by Phil and family. Tommy, Liz, and the kids arrive before Phil leaves, and Jackie Sunshine is on her way. Dad is in rare form, despite announcing that he wants everybody to leave after a scant ten minutes. Having an audience pleases him greatly. That the crowd is his family is a double *mitzvah*, for him and for us all. With all the fluff being chiseled away from his life, all that remains is the love.

"I was seventeen years old," he begins, "and had just completed my first semester of pre-med at Illinois University. Brother Mickey, he returned home wounded from the war. As I've already told you, I was under age so my father, he comes along to enlist me in the Navy fleet marines.

"'I want to kill Germans,' I tell my father."

Ree-ally? We all know Dad has no killer instinct. With the brash protectiveness of a brother, he was simply voicing the wishes of a young upstart whose sibling had suffered the brutality of war.

"*Nu*, so there I am, standing in a room waiting for an exam with four thousand naked men who are enlisting." Surrounded by his children and their children—in chairs nearby, on the floor at his feet, and settled into the folds of the bed covers—he speaks commandingly from his pillows. We crowd together as closely as we can to our Zayde. "We're advised to go sign up for life insurance. Most of us, they warn, won't be returning home." His tale of courage and survival winds a spell around us all.

Nothing is too big for our Zayde to conquer. So what's a little cancer-schmancer?

"I was falsely accused, as it happens, of giving out paraldehyde to men who were alcoholics." Dad seems to expand in size, unfurling the drama and drawing his family more closely into his aura. "To someone who doesn't drink, that colorless liquid gives kind of a buzz. It has a pleasant scent, you know."

"No, Dad, actually we didn't," Jackie says.

"So whaddya think happens next? They throw me in a single-cell brig for a whole day and a half! The two fellas who did what I was accused of," he says, wrapping up the narrative as though completing a successful sales call, "they were sentenced to fifteen years each of hard labor. And that's why after nineteen months of service to my country, I was given an honorable discharge."

Thursday night. I arrive back in Los Angeles to find my father visibly weaker and thinner. "*Nu*, Dad, are you happy?"

"Oh, *yes*," he replies with gusto. "I'm very happy."

"Good. Then I'm happy, too."

Much of the time, I'm *more* than happy. The blessings of these days are so deep that I can hardly sleep at night. Each moment with Dad feels like a condensed course in unconditional love. The father I longed for yet never had is now telling his sons, "I'm so glad Linda's here." Loving him as I have longed to be loved *by* him is healing me. Loving him washes away the illusion of love withheld in my youth. The thought form that my father—well-meaning but imperfect—couldn't give me the love I wanted is being released like a mere memory chronicled in a bedside journal of dreams. The pain of this wretched disease has caused Dad to realize that he loves me dearly, and that he's been wrong to think less of me. The love between us has no limits, no boundaries, no source in this world.

It simply *is*.

Jackie Sunshine arrives, toting a shopping bag of food from Gelson's deli and her usual dose of radiance. The warm turkey sandwich on a fresh sourdough roll sliced in a just-so diagonal way is Dad's favorite treat, and a cranberry-yam dish takes the edge off my hunger. Sprawled across the table, the Scrabble board bears testimony to our recent game. Dad's narrow victory of only twenty points is for me a sort of winning.

"I'm going to lie down now," he announces to Jackson. "You girls play the first game together while I rest up a little."

"Got it, Dad."

"Oh, my," he says almost inaudibly, bracing himself with one hand against the refrigerator. *No-o.* Those are the same words he uttered months ago just before fainting. I grab him instantly and prop him upright until he can stand on his own. Jackson and I try to walk him to bed but he brushes us off like birds pecking at a feeder.

"I can manage by myself," he says with the aborted energy of a power outage in an electrical storm.

Dear Devi,

How are you?

I just listened twice to your voicemail. It makes great sense, and the love in your voice was very dear. It seems I won't be needed here much longer.

This is a blessed time with my father. The dysfunction between us is melting away like a dream that's nearly over. I'm learning so much especially about love and that whatever has happened in the past is being healed simply by loving him unconditionally, which has been happening for many years but now is accelerated.

Dad's accepting my help—a little gruffly, to say the least! But it feels like the Divine Mother is nurturing him through me. He's been on heavy narcotics for three days and is almost completely bed-ridden. My four brothers are reeling from the imminent loss of their father. Yet they're all doing well.

Yesterday, Dad's girlfriend went shopping and bought him some knickknacks for the bathroom. He was so cute, saying, "I'm dying and she's buying me towels?"

The words of Yogananda's disciple Gyanamata come alive as I read them with a slightly different twist. Instead of, "The things that happen to us do not matter; what we become through them does," it's "The things that happen to us do not matter; how we react to them does."

I'm glad to stay in touch with you. The hospice nurse is on her way over, followed by a visit from my rabbi brother and his daughter Sara. It's a busy time!

With love,

Lila

The phone rings as Dad settles into bed. Chana has just returned with her mother from three days in New York. Although born and raised in Los Angeles, the young Jewess has absorbed the undertones of her mother's Bronx accent.

"Zayde, so Mom and I are back."

"That's great, sweetie! How was your trip?"

"Like, I just couldn't find the right shoes. Even with, like, some of the best shopping in the country there! Zayde, can you imagine! So, like, tell me, what are your thoughts?"

"It happens," he says softly.

"Zayde, when we were at a restaurant in Manhattan, I, like, asked the waitress her name. This is something you, like, always do and by your example have taught us to do. So when she came back to our table, I'm all, like, 'Collette, may I have more bread?' And she says to me—Zayde, I'm, like, so-oo totally not kidding—'You remembered my name!' And she was all, like, so happy."

Zayde laughs, places the phone on its cradle, and improvs the conversation for me. He makes a grand story out of it as he does with everything. He enthralls, captivates, and turns us all into children at storytelling time. No one enjoys life like Zayde. *No one.*

There are many moments in these last days with my father when I feel a great peace in my heart. Indeed, his condominium is becoming a shrine filled with a band of angels.

It's late, very late. Actually, it's already the next day. Unable to sleep, I tiptoe down the hallway to stand outside my father's half-open door as I sometimes do. Just to hear the music and miracle of his breath. Inhale, exhale. Over and over. The exhalations are getting longer now, as if by breathing in this manner he might rally the strength to force the cancer from his body cells. How many more breaths remain in his life? *Life is short,* Dad always says, over and over. Inhale, exhale.

When I was younger his words meant so little. Now they mean so much.

The Oakland A's and the Los Angeles Angels baseball game is the backdrop for a tender father-daughter exchange. "You don't know what a *mitzvah* you're doing, Linda, for me to have family staying with me."

"You don't know what a blessing this is for *me*, Dad. I wouldn't be anywhere else. Or have it any other way."

Moshe says that the hardest of the Ten Commandments to observe is about honoring one's parents. I'm not saying that caring for my father with what he calls an insidious disease is a required duty.

I'm saying it's a great privilege.

THE GREAT MEDICATION MYSTERY

I've imagined Dad calling out to me several times lately. With an exacting certainty I'm sure I hear his voice, fainter by the day though ever forceful. Yet when I rush to his door to look in on him, I find him sleeping soundly.

Is it only in my head that I hear him calling out—Linnie?

Later he actually does call to me. "We can do this," he says as I adjust his pillows.

A tiny gesture with a grand intention. I cannot put Dad's life back together or hurl his cancer into oblivion, but I can make his world a little more orderly. And I can show rather than tell him that he is loved beyond imagining. He searches my eyes for the support he dares not ask for outwardly.

It is there, father mine. It will always be there.

"Yes, Dad, we can do this. Together. We're a team."

"Do you want your blintz on a white plate, Dad, or a brown one?" I ask him this morning.

"Doesn't make any difference," he answers matter-of-factly, reading the paper in bed. For Dad to give orders so nonchalantly means he's at peace with himself. Potent life force radiates from his hazel eyes, their brilliance highlighted by the olive-green stripes of his shirt, a plaid flannel he rarely wears. We're waiting for the Vicodin to take effect. Three polyester pillows, stacked neatly behind the straightened bedcovers, prop him up. His voice rings with a joy that conveys many states of being—that he's cared for by his family; that he can relax into his daughter's ministrations to give him a choice of plates for his breakfast blintz; and most supremely, that he's in touch with his soul. Bliss-tears fall from my eyes, unseen by Dad, hazing my view of the simple meal I'm preparing for him.

He shuffles to the table for a quick game of Scrabble to pass the time while we wait for the hospice nurse. Dad makes no pretense of hiding his feelings. He doesn't much care for Eve. With the best of intentions, she always insists he take extra medications—drugs that may as well never have passed through the portals of his condominium. This time with Dad is all about the waiting—for his meds to work, for the caregivers to arrive, and for that moment of final freedom when all waiting will cease.

"The sides aren't browned enough, Linnie." The blueberry blintz, he complains, is not to his liking.

"Sorry, Dad. I can slosh it around in the pan a little longer if you want, yes?"

"You didn't use enough margarine."

My parent inspects the fruit-filled crepe from every angle, poking at it with his fork and rolling it across the chipped white plate as though it had no business being there. The cracked dinnerware, like the bathroom towels, is at least half a century old. My heart delights in knowing a fact of which Dad is unaware. The problem he finds so off-putting is not my cooking, but the cancer spreading throughout his body and decreasing his appetite. It no longer matters to me what Dad says, or that I've never been able to do anything right for him. I'm learning to treasure him in spite of, and precisely for, who he is. Death makes life so precious.

At least my checker-playing is improving. Dad leaves his blintz uneaten and we play a game. He corners my last piece in such a way that all I have to do is not make any hasty moves, and we're tied—which, to the little five-year-old who is still alive within me, is a victory of sorts. Dad's beating me in checkers as a child made me tough, just as having me work my way through university made me independent. All I feel now is gratitude for this man who has been the perfect parent—maybe not the father I wanted but exactly the father I needed.

What's more, I'm happy to see him comfortable in his own home, enjoying the luxury of *kvetching* to his daughter about such trifles as her poorly cooked blintz.

Moshe jaunts in to visit Dad before the hubbub of the weekly Sabbath preparations begin at his house—a flurry of cleaning and cooking and phone calls. He also comes to allow me a much needed health club pilgrimage. We speak on the sofa of many things, our banter spiced with joking. Humor has always been the hallmark of our family. We use it to express our innate sense of fun, to survive our domestic dysfunctions, and—well, just because we can.

Dad has suspected since his first hospital internment last March that the nurses were dipping into his meds. A little Vicodin here, a few pain patches there—what a nice way to supplement a paycheck! *Selling drugs on the black market, or perhaps secretly indulging their own addictions?* I expect my-brother-the-doctor to shed light on the subject and Phil does exactly that, but with a most surprising answer.

"It's true and very common in the medical profession. Happens all the time."

The ongoing drama of Dad's drug supplies disappearing—the powerful narcotics of Vicodin tablets and Fentanyl pain patches—occurs more quickly than my recorded charting of his dosages document.

Thus begins The Great Medication Mystery. At my father's firm prompting and feeling not a little silly, I decide to hide the potent patches in my suitcase.

Lo and behold, my next inventory check confirms that five of the ten patches have disappeared.

And I'm not much help. Dad finds the theatrics of panic and pandemonium highly entertaining. "See? What did I *tell* you, Sister!" he says impishly, his eyes growing more luminous with each mishap. "*Now* who's *meshugenah?*"

Nothing like a good whodunit to create a lively diversion from the cancer. Our detective work is underway. A local locksmith referred by Jackson is enlisted. Everyone agrees that the lock on the front door must be changed—secretly, of course, without telling the neighbors. Now: Who else spends time at Dad's? *Aha!* The hospice workers. The least likely of suspects in their clever ruse of selfless servants to humanity are eyed with base scrutiny.

From now on whenever they arrive, I am ordered to hide all pain medications, some of them on my person. *As if plastic pill bottles bulging from my trouser pockets would be inconspicuous!*

"Linnie, listen to me," Dad says in earnest severity. "These people must *never* be left alone *in the same room* with my medications. We can't trust *anyone*. Do you under*stand*?" My father is one of few people who can actually speak in italics.

"Yes, Dad." I stifle a snicker, tickled to see him so engrossed in the drama. "I understand. You're the boss. Whatever you want is fine by me."

Hidden in the vegetable drawer of the refrigerator are the heavier painkillers and anti-anxiety drugs that concern him hardly at all. Any comfort-producing medications that might rob him of his awareness and sense of control hold no allure.

Next on our list, we review who has a set of keys to Dad's place. *Aha* again! The neighbors down the street. There's Rob on one block, a recovering addict and a dear friend with whom Mom and Dad used to socialize, and Stu on the other, a playwright and bowling enthusiast who always has time to chat whenever he sees Dad. Both are close friends of the family. Both are now under suspicion.

Moshe and I sit in the living room with our feet propped up on the newspapers piled in haphazard stacks on the coffee table, discussing from all angles the absurdity of a dying man being robbed by his neighbors.

"Isn't this whole thing a bit ludicrous, Bro? I mean, it's fun for Dad and all, but you don't think . . ."

Moshe looks at me pointedly, shifting the mood of the conversation. "You know, Sis, when the narcotics started to disappear, I'm *tellink* you, you were suspect."

"You're joking, right? Moshe, tell me you're kidding. This is absolutely inane! I've never heard such unmitigated nonsense."

Perhaps I can divert my brother with a barrage of sophisticated vocabulary. Not the words with high Scrabble points but impressive all the same. My time spent at the game board seems to have served me well. My relaxed smile becomes an awkward grimace, and the room feels suddenly too warm. Does the thermostat need to be reset, I wonder—or did the housekeeper accidentally vacuum up all the breathable air? I shift in my seat. This discomfort is probably how anyone would react on the verge of being labeled a thief and an addict by her own family.

So. This is how my father feels when he'd rather watch baseball than talk!

"It's always the butler," Moshe—looking so like Dad—adds with the poise of one who knows he's right no matter how much evidence exists to the contrary.

"Yes it is, isn't it?" I'm starting to feel a little like a character actor in a melodrama. A little like, the butler?

The disappearance of the narcotics is solved at last. My-brother-the-rabbi was right. I'd miscounted the pain patches, thinking they were ten to a box when instead they had arrived from the pharmacy *in two separate boxes taped together*. There were actually only five to a box, not five that had gone missing from a single box. Neither hospice, the nurses, nor the neighbors were at fault.

The mistaken count was after all my error.

The "Unfinished Business" Sandwich

My Dearest Brothers,

M *y Dearest Brothers,*
      Well, just as I think I'm loving you as much as I can, I find I can love you even more. Each of you, I know, would say the same. This time with Dad is opening our hearts and teaching us the greatest lesson of all—that love has no bounds. We probably all have the same question: when is this test going to end for Dad so that he will suffer no longer? A possible answer came today through the hospice health aide who came to help Dad bathe—Felicity from Ghana, with sixteen years' experience of caring for people who are about to leave this world.

Dad showered while she sat on the bed at his request to be close by and make sure he didn't fall. I asked Felicity when she thought he might pass. She said he just told her he's not ready to go because he needs to bring his family together. Interesting, and very "Dad" because he's told all of us he is ready to go.

It's also significant that he'll share this information with a complete stranger precisely because she's not family and therefore is safe to talk to.

"Your Dad's still strong," Felicity told me. "He'll stay in this world until he does what he needs to do."

Then she added while changing the bed sheets, "People don't pass from this world with unfinished business. They'll linger on despite all odds to accomplish what they set out to do in their lifetime." Guys, she spoke with great certainty, having witnessed this scenario in one family after another. "Oh, I've seen many times that the family fights while the dying person hangs on in tremendous pain and discomfort until all is resolved. I've seen this without exception. Your father will not pass away until his family is healed. He will not leave this world with unfinished business."

Maybe Felicity's right about this man of strength, accomplishment, dignity, and honor. Maybe he won't leave this world until all the rifts within our family are healed. So, my brothers, I ask you: Is there any unfinished family business that we can help Dad to wrap up?

Gotta go now, he wants to play Scrabble. Please share this letter with your wives and children.

With all love,
Favorite Sis

Sundays are always full. So much company, so much love, all of it a little too much now for Dad. Phil and Zach stop by this morning when Dad's at his freshest, intuiting the perfect time to catch the glow of his life at its zenith. He seems energized to see them. My brother-the-doctor repairs Dad's broken CD player that sat for months, defective and unused. Phil can fix anything. Moshe visits with Chana and Sara, then Shmuel and Bracha arrive followed by Tom, Liz, Tessie, and Noah. Everybody piles into Dad's bedroom. Sparks of transluscent joy fly in all directions. Our patriarch leans against the headboard of his bed, bolstered by his pillows and his family. The loved ones to whom he's given life now are giving it back to him.

Dad is still winning at Scrabble, though a little less often. As Phil says, the subtext these days is all about keeping him out of pain. With him eating and drinking so little, the price of more Vicodin is nausea. Managing the cancer pain and the drug symptoms has become a supreme balancing act as the combination of the two begins to blindside his fading body.

For the second day in a row, I hear my father calling out to me. *Am I imagining it?* I think not. Perhaps what I'm hearing is the inward call for help that he refuses to vent outwardly. *Can it be that I'm experiencing my father on deeper levels and "hearing" the soul connection between us?*

In the quiet post-company dining room, Dad looks across the table at his firstborn who is struggling to cut a sandwich in half with a kitchen knife that has long since outlived its usefulness. Much like the foldout sofa, the cutlery too is a joke.

"You're so pretty," he says tenderly. His words surround me like the necklace of my mala.

The fiber of our relationship is being healed, changed, transmuted into pure light. The years of parent-child struggle are waning into the ether like a phonograph needle on an antiquated vinyl record that has reached the end of its final song track. Indeed, I've carved out this incarnation as I've chosen to live it.

HEBREW SCHOOL DOLDRUMS

Why did it take what seemed like ages for me to learn how to tell time? Perhaps because I sensed that once learned, it could never be unlearned. Telling time changes your life forever, the days and decades ahead dictated, driven, determined by the big and little hands of The Mighty Clock with the illusion of time imprinted on one's wrist in the form of a miniature timepiece.

At the same time. another significant event in my life was about to take place. I'd pleaded with my parents for what seemed like an eternity to enroll me in Hebrew school—a crossroads I perceived as a balm for my spiritual sustenance to meliorate my sense of metaphysical malnourishment. For years, questions about God had churned in my impatient mind. *Oy vey, little Linda with her big questions.*

At last the first week of fourth grade commenced. "Linnie, guess what?" Dad beamed his big smile after the clearing of the dinner table. "You start Hebrew classes next week—Tuesdays and Thursdays after school and Sunday mornings."

My nine-year-old heart quickened. *Finally. This is it. This is what I've been waiting for.*

Hebrew school proved to be a mixed blessing. Mrs. Pincus, our middle-aged orthodox teacher, failed to inspire most if not all of her students. Instead, she intimidated us. Any painfully shy student knows that being called on for answers in class is a traumatic ordeal. Mrs. Pincus was one of those teachers who called on us no matter if we raised our hands or not. Whether she did so from a dutiful sense of fairness or by way of keeping us in a state of readiness was inconsequential. My sense of consternation was visceral. In Mrs. Pincus' class, I simply could not relax.

The instructor was a stocky woman, frightfully old and odiferously stale. She dressed the way she taught: in a crisp off-white blouse, mid-calf-length black skirt, and well-worn orthopedic shoes, all lacking any sense of fashion. A cropped black wig—befitting an espoused Jewess though a shade too dark for her skin—sat on top of her head mimicking a bird's nest in the highest branches of a gnarled oak tree. It gave her an unnaturally sallow appearance, whisking across her forehead in waves of synthetic curls. Mrs. Pincus was short in stature. Even so, she loomed over the breadth of the classroom with a gaze that was both menacing and foreboding. *Does this woman truly hold the answers to the most pressing spiritual questions that churn in my mind?*

My one saving grace was that all twenty children were seated alphabetically. Thus could Zaret, Linda hide in the back row, followed only by Zingerman, Judy. If I slouched at just the right angle and retracted my aura more snugly around my skinny little personage, I found I could go unnoticed. Most important of all, as I learned the hard way: *don't make eye contact with the teacher.* That was tantamount to *asking* to be called on. The trick was to remain hidden from her field of vision by shifting ever so slightly, imperceptibly behind the students seated in the front row. Other helpful tips that I discovered through trial and error: don't fiddle with the ribbon on your ponytail; don't scratch your nose even if it itches like crazy; and don't for any reason whatsoever lift your hands above your shoulders. The ever-watchful Mrs. Pincus could misconstrue these gestures as a desire to actually *want* to answer a question. In front of *everyone.*

I would rather die.

"Does anyone know how to tell a Jew from a non-Jew?" Mrs. Pincus' dictatorial tone failed to inspire the rows of little people incarcerated in her classroom, probably all of us there against our will and better judgment. Not one of us wanted to respond.

No one dared raise a hand. A few of the children looked at each other, hoping to see a solution magically appear on one of their classmates' foreheads.

"The answer is simple." Mrs. Pincus inhaled sharply to discipline her words as well as her students. "Only Jews can properly enunciate the *ch* sound. Let's try it together." A dismissive flick of her wrist put the subject to rest. Again the students looked at each other. Like the fabled *Emperor's New Clothes*, no one wanted to be exposed as a fool, unable to produce the correct sound and thereby labeled an inferior Jew. Or worse yet, a Gentile.

Some of my fellow prisoners spat, others coughed. Somehow we all managed to say our throaty *ch*'s reasonably well.

If it is indeed true that there are no bad stories and only bad storytellers, Mrs. Pincus wasn't so hot. Jewish history class for me offered no enchantment. It resembled a page of dry aged parchment paper with all the texture wrung out of it. Yet studying the Ten Commandments struck a deep place within the soil of my consciousness. It would be many years until I came to understand them in a truer form:

> *Let nothing tempt you ever to compromise an ideal. Morality is not a question of convention. The Ten Commandments are engraved in human nature on tablets of light. The true reason why theft, violence, murder, and other crimes are wrong is that they hurt first of all the perpetrator himself, condemning him to ever-deeper dungeon levels in the rock fortress of his egoism. If you arm yourself, however, with truthfulness, honesty, and integrity, you will emerge someday into perfect soul-freedom.*[7]

One particular historic event did catch my attention, one considered pivotal to Judaic law. Moses, as the story went, descended the mountain to the Israelites after a forty-day absence. Miscounting his return by a single day, the Jewish people faltered in their faith by constructing the idolatrous golden calf. As it is written, the Lord smote them. And smote them hard. So great was their transgression that it's said even to this day, God punishes those of Judaic faith for the spiritual crime of dishonoring the Second Commandment: *Thou shalt have no other gods before Me.*

The concept of a wrathful God who smote, judged, and punished made me uncomfortable. I could understand my father in a smiting mood after returning from a challenging day of sales, a commission-based job on which he had to feed a wife and five kids. And I could easily imagine Mrs. Pincus smiting me for giving a wrong answer in class even when my hand wasn't raised. *But a God who smites?* Years later I was to learn a deeper significance of this historic and metaphysical event, as it is explained on my spiritual path that embraces original yogic principles:

> *Idol worship means worshipping anything other than God: money, sex, power, fame, sensory pleasures. That was what the golden calf represented, which those Jews worshiped who had fallen into delusion while Moses was up on the mountain, communing with God.* [8]

With its many gods and goddesses, Hinduism is often misunderstood as a polytheistic religion, when instead the Hindu deities represent many aspects of the one God. They personify *ideals* rather than *idols*. Their purpose is to serve as different focal points for a rich variety of devotional expressions. This and more, the future Jewish yogi in fourth-grade Hebrew class would one day come to know.

To her credit as a teacher, Mrs. Pincus wasn't all bad. Learning to read and write Hebrew in her classroom thrilled my heart to its daughter-of-Israel core.

The language of the Jewish people in biblical times was strangely familiar to me. I would later understand through my study of reincarnation that I'd probably spoken Hebrew in former lives. How I loved to trace the peculiarly beautiful letters with my index finger from right to left across the page in a journey of pure joy! A dignified language of antiquity, it rose up from my schoolbook in eager greeting. Reading "ema come, abba go"—the basic Hebraic equivalence level of "see Spot run"—commanded my full attention.

Yet it was in choir that my soul took flight, a voyage expressed in the words of a mystical poem by my Guru that I would read many years later: *"I want to hear Thy still voice, ever singing in the silence of my soul."*[9] I could hear that voice in Cantor Stein's resonant tenor trill so perfectly placed that it seemed to arise from everywhere and nowhere in the classroom. *This, I thought, is the sound of devotion.*

As the Cantor sang, both a spiritual longing and a fullness within me stirred in recognition. *This is what I'm seeking—a direct experience of God through meditation and service.* My silent prayer echoed the words of my Guru-to-be: "Give me Thyself that I may give Thee to all."

Oh no, not again. Another instructor who called on students with their hands down at their sides, exhibiting none of the body language that would give him cause to call on them!

I sat frozen in my seat. Because Cantor Stein sang with such a fine voice, he deserved every benefit of the doubt. Somehow I'd managed to go unnoticed for months in his classroom—proof that my hard work with Mrs. Pincus had served me well. *Maybe he was simply trying to be fair and not exclude anyone?*

One day on a whim, I decided to dress up for Sunday school. The full moon the night before caught me enduring the torture of sleeping with my straggly brown hair in pin-curls. A cascade of ringlets bounced below my thin shoulders upon removing the bobby pins the following morning. Hardly inconspicuous was the yellow cotton blouse with three-quarter-length sleeves under a bright turquoise jumper with its zigzag-stitched pockets—hand-me-downs from an older cousin.

I sat in the back row of Cantor Stein's class, not from the benign grace of alphabetical order, but from a self-imposed desire for obscurity precipitated by a full-blown case of terminal shyness. Even so on that particular Sunday, the Cantor pointed directly at me. My backbone turned to marmalade. Clearly I'd chosen the wrong day to wear this outfit. *What was I thinking?* The bobbing curls and bright colors must have given him the impression that I was practically begging to be called on.

Please God, pick someone else. Not me, not me.

"Stand up, if you would, and sing."

Lord: if I was mistaken about You in my innocent and untested wisdom and You are in fact a God who smites, then smite away. Never has the moment for such punishment been so utterly welcomed.

The Cantor looked down at the roll call list. Of course he didn't know me by name. How could he? I had managed to keep myself invisible in his class for months. Besides, looking down at anything wasn't easy for Cantor Stein, a gesture prohibited by his girth. My mind morphed into a black hole the color of Mrs. Pincus's wig, hearing my chair scrape the floor as I pushed it aside to stand up. I aligned one vertebrae on top of the other by way of gathering strength, certain that I stood on the brink of my own execution. The perspiration on my scalp dampened my ringlets. My throat tightened, refusing to let a trail of air caress the lyrics that would soon cascade forth like the curls around my collapsed shoulders.

From a distant corner of the room that seemed removed from my classmates by light years, I somehow muddled through the melodic Hebrew song so newly learned. My feigned vibrato gained power from the pair of wobbly knees shaking beneath the hem of my jumper. Sometimes when fear overtakes you with complete abandon and disregard for the steadiness of your nerves, it then drops you on the other side of the precipice where only peace resides. Several notes into the song, it carried me to that place.

Silence.

"Nicely done, Miss Zaret." The Cantor pronounced my surname wrong by accenting the last syllable. Stiffly I took my seat. A wave of mortification washed over my warm cheeks, and I couldn't help wondering if for the rest of my life they'd remain permanently flushed. I looked down at the watch that sloshed on my wrist like a hand-me-down I would someday grow into. Its hands, big and little, seemed to hold my very soul. A mere three minutes had passed. There would be no execution, no falling from a precipice. And no smiting.

Not long after, I asked my parents to withdraw me from Hebrew school. Try though I might, I felt I'd advanced as far as I could with my studies. I was nine years old. It was time to move on.

Mine was a journey from religion to spirituality. From Jewess to yogi. From bagels to curry.

ASTRAL ASCENSION

"Last March, my brothers and I learned that our father Aaron Oscar Zaret had advanced Stage 4 pancreatic cancer."

I read these notes several days after Dad's Orthodox Jewish funeral at his astral ascension ceremony, a service performed at Ananda for our loved ones who have passed. Its purpose is twofold: to support the soul of the deceased on its journey accompanied by our loving prayers, and to help those left behind to transmute their loss and give them a sense of closure.

I continued. "After saying good-bye to his loved ones and struggling valiantly for some remaining quality of life, Dad's five-and-a-half-month battle ended with his passing in Los Angeles last Sunday. Five children, ten grandchildren, and two great-grandchildren with another on the way survive him. He remained our father until he left this world, always with love and care. He prepared us for his departure by repeatedly saying how lucky he was, what a wonderful life he'd had, and how blessed he felt to have such a fine family.

"I spent several months as his caregiver. A week ago, I felt strongly that it was time for me to return to Ananda. My departure from Los Angeles allowed my brothers to step in and gave me the opportunity to celebrate Swamiji's sixtieth anniversary of discipleship to Paramhansa Yogananda. My rabbi brother stayed with Dad for two nights. This afforded him the blessing of spending his last Sabbath with his-son-the-rabbi by way of reinforcing his ties with Judaism for the first time since my mother's passing seven years ago.

"The following night, my doctor brother came to stay with Dad. He refused pain medication despite protests from my brother in order to have a more conscious passing. To the very end, my father kept his mental faculties and his fierce independence. Until his last breath he maintained his dignity."

Following this reading I addressed these words to the friend-filled temple: "It's special that you're all here for two reasons. First because you're my family and have come to honor my father as a part of this greater family, and second, because as a woman I wasn't allowed to speak last Sunday at my father's orthodox Jewish funeral.

"Dad was an amazing, fun person, filled with integrity. He was competitive, mainly against himself, always striving to do his best. He was decisive; once he made a decision he put his whole energy behind it. He was mentally focused, as his buddies in cards and Scrabble would testify. He was a loving father, grandfather, and great-grandfather as well as a friend even to strangers. My father abounded in these life-affirming ways of being: a sense of fun, a love of adventure, and an endless repertoire of songs, dances, and stories. Not coincidentally, the main character in most of his stories was himself. Because Dad found himself so infinitely fascinating, others were inclined to view him likewise. His great interest in people led him to hone his people skills, making him an excellent judge of human nature. It's no wonder that he was able to support a large family on a salesman's salary.

"Life itself was his temple. He worshipped at its altar with a rare sense of appreciation.

"Dad was deeply religious in Judaism, yet he lived by his own rules, including the one we kept hidden from our rabbi brother —playing poker on the Friday night Sabbath. He was a man of high standards and accomplishments and held deep respect for people, especially waiters and waitresses, always helping others feel better about themselves. *And he loved his family.* We were his *sadhana*, his identity, his pride, his legacy.

"Aaron was the youngest of seven children, preceded by four brothers and two sisters. He was born in the slum district of Chicago. He would tell us stories of sleeping three to a bed, 'not counting the cockroaches,' with everyone sharing a single bathroom. Ever the *bon vivant* in his youth, Zeke—as he was nicknamed—ranked second of sixty couples in a jitterbug contest. He would dance with two women at a time, keeping one of them airborne, by inventing his own version of the two-step. Graduation from high school came a year early for my father, who read a book a day. He left a pre-med program at the age of twenty to support his mother after his father died. Always he remained positive and cheerful.

"When his older brother returned from the Battle of the Bulge in World War II—injured and decorated with a purple heart medal—Zeke decided that he wanted to fight for his country. He never shipped overseas; instead his heightened sense of competence was grounds for an assignment as a Navy medic to run a sixty-six-bed locked psycho ward. It was then that my father signed up for the first atom bomb test in the Pacific Ocean's Bikini Atoll. A singular act of fate deigned that the commanding officer himself removed my father's name from the enrollment list. Zeke was devastated. All the same, he remained positive and cheerful. As discovered nearly a decade later, all ten thousand men who had enlisted in that assignment returned home completely sterile.

"Then he met my mother, formerly the captain of her high school swimming team. When she beat his brother in a race at Lake Michigan with the weaker advantage of the backstroke, Aaron fell in love. That love lasted fifty-one years. Tennis was my parents' favorite sport, their finesse as mixed doubles partners amply confirmed by two shelves of local tournament trophies. When one of my more competitive brothers once asked Dad why he played the game with Mom—since he was clearly the better of the two—he replied, 'I sacrificed my game to strengthen my marriage.' With a family of young children to raise, my father appealed to my well-to-do grandfather for the financial backing to complete medical school and become a doctor, a lifelong dream still uppermost in his mind. 'No one ever helped me,' my mother's father answered. 'Why should I help you?' Yet Dad as always remained cheerful and positive.

"When life handed him lemons, he made the best lemon ade ever.

"Dad became the top salesman for a major surgical supply company. Thus my brothers and I grew up in a houseful of Ace bandages and other surgical supplies, which explains why we always trick-or-treated at Halloween bandaged from head to toe as mummies. Dad received notable recognition for nineteen percent of nationwide sales for a particular kind of doctor's examination table.

"Then one day without notice, he was fired for being successful —and Jewish. Yet even when the company's anti-semitism caused his dismissal, he remained positive and cheerful. That same day, he secured another job that lasted nearly thirty years.

"My brothers and I were raised in an upper-middle-class suburb of Detroit. Dad would talk about his children like cards in a winning poker hand. In order of age there was me, the international author and business entrepreneur; his-son-the-doctor, an osteopath in private practice who specialized in addiction; his son-the-dot-com mogul; his-son-the-orthodox-rabbi who oversees campus outreach at UCLA; and his-son-the-lawyer who has served many clients well with their personal injury needs. Dad loved to call us his dynasty. Next January, his third great-grandchild will be born.

"Then came the cancer. Always the people person and unfalteringly cheerful, my father bragged incessantly to the hospice staff who visited his bedside. Once when a nurse took his vital signs and monitored his pain medication, she asked, 'Do you have any other questions?' In a voice barely audible he replied, 'Yes, Adelaide, can you sing?'

"My father passed from this world last Sunday morning at 2 a.m. He was buried twelve hours later. Jewish orthodoxy favors a quick burial, stating that the soul has already returned to God and likewise the body must follow.

"*For you are dust and to dust shall you return.*' (Genesis 3:19)

"My family will observe the Jewish practice of sitting *shiva* for a full week, attended by my brothers in honor of their father according to Jewish law to help his soul as it transitions to Heaven.

"Judaism says the soul leaves the body through the ground. Yoga says it leaves through the point between the eyebrows, ideally with the body in a seated position—which was his exact posture when he exited his bodily temple. Death itself found my father embracing the chosen beliefs of each of his children.

"In closing, Zeke was a singer, a dancer, and a storyteller. Surely in Heaven he has become his own song and dance. He will remain forever in our hearts as his own outrageous story."

Jump-Starting the Life Force

Good. Some errands to get me out of the house and out of my mental rut.

Café Eilat is reviewed as a fine kosher restaurant, and the two-block walk helps to clear my head. Dad's explicit instructions to me are, "Linda, get me a seven-grain roll and the soup-of-the-day." We're trying to find something that appeals to his waning sense of taste—anything enjoyable beyond the first two bites. This stage of "the disease" means he likes the thought of food but not the taste of it.

The Israeli girl behind the counter has skin the color of olive wood and raven hair stuffed into a messy ponytail. She asks above the din of a sea of lunch conversations, "What can I get for you?" The hardwood floor and low ceiling amplify the drone of voices and the scraping of chairs as people rise to leave their tables.

"Pardon?" I ask.

"Can I help you?" She flicks the back of her hand with a windshield-wiper motion to shift the bangs and the hurriedness from her eyes.

"I'd like a cup of vegetable soup to go, please. One-third vegetables, two-thirds broth." *Just the way Dad likes it.*

Then come the tears, like being caught in a flash storm without an umbrella. The girl stares at me oddly. How can I explain, *this is for my dying father?*

After a brief nap and a baseball game on television, Dad takes a bite of the sandwich I prepared according to his explicit instructions—a drizzle of mustard, a crisp piece of lettuce, the Eilat roll, and from the kosher market next door, a slice of turkey pastrami.

But it's no use. Dad has no appetite—cravings but no actual hunger. Such anomalies are a natural part of this stage of the cancer, the hospice booklet explains. With all his might, Dad is trying to jumpstart his life force with whatever form of nourishment appeals to his body so that he can remain its resident.

"Hold my hand, Linnie," Dad asks as I leave the room.

I take his hand in mine, long enough to pray that God nourish him with a heaping portion of divine love.

Dear Phil,

What a joy it was to see you and the family yesterday! I kid you not.

There's an unfounded rumor that I'm avoiding Victor's care of Dad for financial reasons. Financial reasons? Can you please squelch this nonsense? Frankly, the reason I don't want Victor is because Dad doesn't want Victor. To have Dad's willpower overrun when he's working through so much right now would be a needless burden for him. He doesn't want paid care, and I think it's finally sinking in that he's stuck with me.

With Love,

Fave Sis

Brother Moshe can be outrageously funny, all the more so for being a source of unconventional humor at the most unexpected moments. When I ask him a question he prefers not to answer, he replies, "If I tell you, I'm going to have to kill you." *Oy.* Unorthodox humor from an orthodox rabbi?

"You know, Sis," he says more seriously, "your brothers are better than you at letting Dad's impatience roll off their backs. Ya just gotta toughen up a little, ya know? You need to not let him get to you like this. Whaddya think?"

"Maybe you're right, Moshe. Sure, that makes sense. What can I say, I'll try to do better."

I want to reach across the chasm of the sofa to embrace my brother and the dearness within him, but the orthodoxy declares that it is forbidden for a sister to touch her brother. Instead I hold him in the silence of my soul.

I must admit, though, my brother asks good questions.

"Zayde, what do you think is Linda's strongest quality?" Moshe asks at Dad's bedside.

"She has heart."

Hearing these words from my father, that heart melts.

One sees in a dying person just before his passing a burst of energy that precedes the soul's transition to the astral world. It may in fact appear that he's rallying and might be able to remain in this world a little longer despite a body that's nearing its expiration date. Perhaps it's not only the person's soul shining through—though that too is a part of the dying process—but also a shifting of footing from this plane of existence to the next.

Maybe for Dad the work is done and the battle is over. Yet how easily his loved ones can misread the signs, and understandably so. How wonderful if our family could understand his process. We're getting a sneak preview of where our Zayde is going and the joy that awaits him.

Dad's energy continues to shift away from this world. His eyes are inaccessibly distant yet filled with light. Being no longer sustained by food can only mean that he's drawing nourishment from the light of his soul, a phenomenon beauteous to behold. Several times today, he asks to hold my hand. Though he won't take my hand for support to walk to the bathroom from his bed. Each time he calls for my help, I feel inwardly to remain silent and send him blessings. Perhaps my spiritual path allows me to

represent to him both what he is leaving and where he is going—
the love of family on the one hand and the bliss of Spirit on the
other. Indian scripture teaches that a person can make consider-
able spiritual progress toward the end of an incarnation. *Might this
imply that his loved ones can also make great strides alongside him?*

Doubling Dad's pain patch means no more Vicodin. Alas, the
tradeoff is dearly paid for with significant personality changes
that render him more intense, abrupt, impatient. Whatever I
do for him once again is wrong. Since returning to Los Angeles
twelve days ago, for the second time I've become ill, my body
splintered and ragged at the seams. *I can do this, God. Or rather
You can do this through me. We're a team.*

Dad's favorite hospice worker just arrived. Tina struts around
the bedroom gutsy and confident, her pastel pink nurses' uniform contrasted with the rich shades of her dulcet dark skin. The
beaded cornrows adorning her face swing freely like Christmas
ornaments on pine tree branches. Tina sneaks a glance at herself
in the full-length closet door mirror, then with knowing approval
smiles back at her reflection. She and Dad have already discussed
the new Republican vice-president running mate, the Florida
hurricane evacuation, repercussions of the recent inflation, and
simple remedies for alleviating dry mouth. Their laughter ebbs
and flows in raucous waves.

"Tell me you love me, Zeke." The hospice worker hides a
giggle in the cradle of her palm. She strokes his tiny hand and

assumes a theatric pose on the edge of the bed as though entertainment is a part of her job description.

"Tina," he asks, "does your husband know you're in bed with another man?"

With Dad in the shower I ask her the same question as Felicity: "How long?"

"I can usually tell." She tosses a sideways peek in the mirror. "But your father's putting on such a good show to hide behind, girl, I have no idea."

"*Sssh.* Are you sure?" I whisper so Dad won't hear.

"Honest, Hon. I can't tell with this guy. Your Dad's quite a character!" Tina shakes her cornrows, sending fairy dust flying from her angelic form.

For the first time ever, I give Dad a haircut. He expresses concern that his hair, uncommonly thick and pure white in color, is now thinned and brittle to the touch. All the primping and fussing over him I'd like to say is touching. A sweet and tender father-daughter moment.

"Dad, do you want me to go home?"

"*No-o,* Dolly! Why would you even *say* such a thing?"

"Because you've been yelling at me all day."

Why have all of Dad's emotions bottle-necked into a cauldron of simmering wrath? Neither cushioning nor patience fuel his words. Only raw anger. A man especially from my father's generation can express an entire range of feelings through this singular emotion. Whatever he is experiencing within his great intensity of feeling, I cannot even begin to understand. Is it intentionally directed at me, or am I just caught in the crossfire? I suspect the latter. Oddly, Dad's vented rage seems to hold a certain purity. *Is it a coincidence that this all began last night after I slipped out for a few hours?*

"I have cabin fever, Dad. If you don't mind, I need to go out for a bit."

"This is too much for you, taking care of me." He mutters under his breath, more to himself than to me.

Dad's right. Once again he sees right through me. Yet if we try to talk this out, I know he'll simply send me home.

Earlier in front of Jackson, he reprimanded me harshly. "I can see you haven't learned yet about not talking on the phone," he barked. "How many times do I have to tell you? *Linda, you're wasting valuable time.*"

Indeed, all time now must seem supremely valuable to him. My father is a driven man who likewise drives his children—to excellence, to higher standards, to greater accomplishments. Whether we want it or not, whether it's who we are or not, carries little weight. Sometimes, though, he drives us all crazy. Even so, I wish in my very cells that he would stay in this world to drive me crazy forever.

Surely Dad feels badly for keeping me here—and most of all for needing my help to begin with. This, he defines as weakness. The more the cancer takes hold of him, the more he fights against its accompanying infirmity. In that state of being are housed all the qualities my father abhors—powerlessness, helplessness, loss of control. The thought of being pitiable is, well, pitiful to him. If he were some glorious wild animal, this is the moment he'd be walking off into the woods to die, his dignity intact. Instead he gets angry—not at Tina or at any of the other caregivers but at me. Why? *Because we're close enough that he can express his most guarded feelings.* These tactics may work for him but they leave me numb and smarting.

It seems that a romanticized happily-ever-after charmed finale to my relationship with my father won't be happening in this lifetime. What has transpired between us is over; what hasn't happened, now never will. Within my spiritual training lies my sole resolution. It teaches gratitude never blame; graciousness never grudge-holding.

Dad can barely finish our Scrabble game. He scarcely eats or drinks all day. Along with his pills, he swallows a packaged nutritional drink and two teaspoons of soup without interest or appetite, as though they too are medicinal.

Brothers Jackie and Tommy are on their way over.

"It's too late for visitors, guys." Dad shifts restlessly in his bed.

"Five minutes, Pops, just give us five minutes," Tommy pleads, his courtroom skills serving him well to win this case.

Such a sweet visit, Dad and his boys. How he loves to see his boys.

And what of Aaron's daughter?

Sometimes people ask me, by way of making more than small talk and genuinely trying to understand the ebbs and flows of my life, "So, do you have any children?"

"Yes," I reply, "twenty. And I keep them in bottles."

In its own way, my company Spirit-in-Nature Essences has made my father proud. The oldest flower essence line outside the United Kingdom where flower essences first originated, these twenty vibrational tinctures have helped countless thousands of people of all ages, pets, and even plants to attain "perfect well-being" as our byline suggests. My entrepreneurial work has always impressed Dad. It also helped him learn to live with my life choices, even though I was supposed to marry the doctor, the lawyer, or the rabbi and have a houseful of kids *not* kept in bottles.

A part of Dad is emerging that is more unconditionally accepting and wanting the best for his children— meaning what *we* want to do with our lives instead of what *he* wants for us. Through my strength of will often hard-won, I've managed to find my own way despite the prescriptions imposed on me by my parents. As for the challenges they gave me, I'm grateful.

My father is growing. It hasn't been easy for him.

Tina makes the bed with newly washed sheets of assorted floral patterns while Dad showers, unassisted and refusing any help. If the sheets' thread count was three hundred when they were first purchased, by now it's probably down to thirty.

The hospice angel pats down the bed as though it were alive and needed reassurance. "You tell me if I can get you anything, Zeke."

"You're the boss, girl. And you tell me if *you* need anything."

"Got it, buddy. Just make sure you don't fall in there. I don't want you makin' no more work for these old bones." The cover sheet in her hands billows above the bed like a hot air balloon hovering over a meadow.

"Tina, is your husband a big baseball fan?" Dad asks.

"No, but he's *my* biggest fan." The hospice aide clucks at her own sassiness.

With her duties completed, the front door clicks shut behind the cornrows in the pink uniform like an abruptly ended sentence.

Dad calls me to his side. "Linda, come here. Hold my hand."

My father's hand is cold to the touch. I look into his eyes. He turns away, wanting contact yet nothing too intimate, too close. *I'm here for you, Dad. Please know I'm so here for you.* His eyes tear. Whatever is happening within him is inaccessible, locked away in a silence beyond words. While I'm privileged to share these last days with him, no one is allowed into the private chamber where he's preparing to leave this world and everyone dear to him.

"Dad, you're so handsome." I choke on a lump of emotion while trying to disguise it, knowing how distasteful these outer displays of sentiment are to him.

Aaron's worldly cares are over. The blood pressure, blood thinning, and high cholesterol are no longer of concern. Nor are his goals, dreams, accomplishments. Even with the pained look on his cancer brow, Dad looks like a young man.

He looks like someone who is beginning his life, not ending it.

There's nothing to fear because of course he has the strength and courage to deal with whatever comes. He's done it many times before. He's always survived, probably a million times.

SABBATH CANDLES, SCRABBLE TILES

The clustered stone houses rising out of the Umbrian hillsides appear not so much built as hatched. Perhaps they spring organically from the ground, invisible one day and fully birthed the next. Much like the hillsides, the Italian language is soft with its nurturing garland of vowels that carries the dearness of the heart and of this country. Here my travels have taken me within the devotional aura of the Ananda Assisi community, rated one of the best yoga retreats in all of Europe.

My seventeen-year-old 1998 Seicento is a joke. Driving it is a form of austerity. Its frog-green iridescence lends a shimmering and lifelike eeriness to its metallic spine. The car hops lithely over the poorly patched country roads, an older vehicle with new tires to somehow neutralize its aging process. Over the past few months, I've been five times to the mechanic who sometimes tells me after waiting an hour (enough time to change my guitar strings) that the new muffler—new at least to my car—hasn't yet arrived. *Fiat* as a friend explained stands for: Fix It Again, Tony.

On the drive home from Gualdo Tadino, I pass an *anziana* whose weathered face resembles a landscape with a smile, brandishing the elements of earth, water, wind, fire. She wears a babushka and earth-colored clothes and sturdy walking boots that have trudged through many seasons. She tips from side to side like a broken doll plowing forward, as though she's borrowed someone else's thick legs from the knees down. Life has been hard and life has been good. Perhaps she's lost a child too soon or a husband too late. Perhaps she's known a lack of richer food and drink and many of life's fineries. But the dear *anziana* lumbers on the shoulder of the road, walking the earth to her final destination, her own shoulders stooped from stirring a pot on the stove or tending a little one in her arms.

I've always thought people talked about the weather because they had nothing better to say. Here in Umbria, I talk about the weather all the time. Partly because it's within my Italian language skills to do so with some measure of eloquence, and because Umbria has no fitting translation for the perfect word to best describe it—*bellissimo*? Chatting up the weather gives perspective to one's views as well as being a fairly cosmic topic. Breathtaking is this *paese* filled with an Italian passion that expresses itself through Mother Nature in Her chameleon garb of climate. Her behavior is outspoken, bombastic, without boundaries or definitions. What colors will She chose next on the nearby hillsides and distant mountains, like my mother with her crayons?

In the wintertime, snowflakes fly in three directions at once: sideways, diagonal, and vertical to the ground. The other seasons know hail, rain, downpours, drizzles. The weather is whimsical, operatic, emotional to a fault. The sunsets blaze in the heavens, each one consciously varied in its nightly festival of colors. Sometimes the sun shimmies behind a billowing of clouds. Watching the Umbrian sky is like witnessing the scribbling of a poem across one's soul.

The poetry of Dad's life is tucked away in my cells. Only now, seven years after his passing, am I beginning to realize throughout the context of our family—with its complexity, dysfunction, and dearness—just what kept my father around for so long with unfinished business.

His daughter.

"You got good hands, baby," Dad says as I rub his back. He who rarely initiates physical contact asks for a massage. He wants nothing to do with the comforts associated with being an invalid, and so I am not allowed to swab his cracked mouth with a sponge stick or cool his forehead with a damp washcloth. But a backrub is okay by him.

Now we're back to the Scrabble board because Dad lost last time.

A note left on the doorstep by a neighbor catches my eye when I step outside to retrieve the morning newspaper, the door mat under my toes feeling like the unwashed coat of a mixed breed of terrier.

Dear Zeke,

I'm Terry, your neighbor with red hair. When I saw you the other week, I knew you were sick. I realize I'm always so busy that I don't know my neighbors. How sad.

Please, if I can help you in any way, like going to the store, let me know. I'll leave you my number. I have always appreciated your elegance and smile. I will pray for you.

Your name comes from Ezekiel in the Hebrew Bible. It means "God will strengthen." I pray that God will strengthen you.

Terry

I cannot do this any longer. I can no longer tolerate the yelling. Dad might be around for a while yet and even if not, I've done all I can for him. It will be better for me to serve him from my own home where I can stay centered and send prayers rather than remain here where I'm ill, shaking, and thoroughly wrung out. Helping Dad to die is more difficult than junior high school gym class where I would execute a backward somersault on the six-inch-wide balance beam with my teammates standing by to spot me. Now only God is my spotter.

And I cannot play any more Scrabble. *Please Lord, no more Scrabble.*

With a candid simplicity, the Indian scriptures elucidate the most complex of human emotions. My Guru's Guru explains that the emotion of anger is caused by thwarted desire. Dad is using fierce coping mechanisms to deal with his dying process, his wrath with each passing day flaming to brighter shades of fury. This is *his* life and no one has the right to take it from him. Not even God. *Who does He think He is, anyway? What is He, nuts?*

Anger rages in Aaron's veins with a fire that he vents freely to his daughter. Whether it's directed at me, someone else, or no one in particular: it's time for me to leave.

I must say good-bye, knowing I may never see my father again. God will have to give me the strength to do this. *In fact, I think He already has.*

"I'm very mad at you, Linda, for saying that I treat Tina better than you." So *that's* why he's been yelling at me constantly.

"But…"

"Nothing is more important than family. I was very hurt by that."

"It was a joke, Dad. I was just kidding."

"Don't joke." He responds with the directness of one whose words like dance steps are always carefully placed. "Why would you even *say* such a thing?" What I can't seem to explain that caused the misunderstanding in the first place isn't that I'm envious of how he treats Tina. It's about why he cannot treat his daughter with the same kindness he extends to an outsider.

"Linda, I'm not myself." This admission is as close as my father can approach to an apology. From him, it *is* an apology.

"Dad, do you remember our earlier conversation of several months ago when I said you were harsh and verbally abrasive with me?"

"I'm sorry," he whispers. "I know I'm not an easy person. Now I know why I'm staying around so long." He takes my hand. "It's to tell you how much I love you."

"Dad, I'm going to fly home," I say quietly. "It's time to go and besides, my business needs me."

"I understand, Linnie, you go home. I can see by your actions what a fine person you are. Your sticking with me through all of this is proof."

In this moment something shifts. A father-daughter rift is healed. *If only I can take a little more time for self-care during the day, then I won't have to leave even for a night's respite.*

"Dad, it's so hard for me to see you struggle like this. I'm here to help you get to Heaven, and I can't do my job if you keep getting angry with me."

"Dolly, where's the remote? I don't see it. Can you turn on the baseball game?"

Too much talk. Wa-ay too much talk.

News of Sarah Palin's torrential charisma splashes across the front page when Dad unfolds the morning paper. "I made a bet with Moshe that the Democrats are gonna win this election. If I'm not around, Linda, be sure your brother gives you a nickel for me."

That nickel now sits in a tiny decorative envelope in a box with other family keepsakes.

At sundown we honor the Sabbath, a day of rest and rejoicing blessed by Hashem. "Why tonight, Dad? It's not like we light candles every week. Or *ever*."

"I haven't lit candles since your ma's been gone. I'm doing it because you're here. And because Moshe asked me to."

Leeby calls early today as she often does just before the sun buries itself in the hills of Jerusalem where she's raising her family and where for thousands of years devout souls have traveled for sacred pilgrimage, much like the *anziana* who lives each day until it disappears into the dimming twilight.

"Zayde?" asks her three-year-old son. "Do you have a booboo?"

"Oh yes, Yehuda," Zayde replies softly, his eyes aflame like Sabbath candles that flicker in a mystical world. "I have a *big* booboo."

Good-Bye, Linnie

Dad has not eaten for six days. Two bites of a bagel with cream cheese and one candy-sized ice cream sampler are all he can manage. He is living on the pure strength of his soul in a body no longer regenerated by food—a hard realization for any family, but even more so for a Jewish one! The prescribed rounds of oxygen today for the first time hold greater appeal to him. A gentle hum from the machine emanates from the closed closet, the plastic tube in his nostrils being the only evidence that he can no longer breathe easily on his own. I awaken Dad from his nap. He startles. Journeying as though from a distant land, one now more familiar to him than this world, he returns to his body.

Brother Tommy, fresh from a treadmill workout, brings his son to visit. The five-year-old bundle of kinesthetic energy jumps on Dad's bed, rumples the sheets, and dives into his grandfather's arms.

"Noah," I ask him, "do you have anything to say to Zayde?"

"I love you, Zayde," he twinkles.

Zayde smiles.

Again and again, Aaron tells his sons, "Do a good job." This is the message he inscribes—unwillingly and with much prompting—in the book of Judaic law he bequeathed to Shmuel. Such gestures he considers mere sentimentality. In his mental dictionary the words *melodrama* and *mush* are assigned the same definition.

Encouraging Dad to finish his pain meds takes all of ten minutes. He sits on the side of his bed mildly dazed and disoriented, reticent to inject the blood-thinning serum into the black-and-blue folds of his abdomen. He trains me to do this for him, loath to concede to my insistence, all the while refusing to accept my help. *Me*, a convicted fainter at a blood draw, giving *shots?* Once finished, he relaxes his needle-battered stomach and lays back on the perfectly stacked pillows. His eyes lose their focus and roll upward.

"Good night, Dad."

"I love you, I love you. Good-bye, Linnie," he says and then corrects himself: "Good night." *Perhaps he actually means to say good-bye?*

Or thinks he won't be awakening from his sleep.

By 1 a.m. to no avail I've tossed, turned, and thrashed between the sheets. Sleep is shunning my company, and it seems only a mindless video on my laptop can disengage me from this earthly drama. Clearly my father is no longer being sustained by food, air, or water. Likewise by association with him, neither am I.

A new day. Dad is restless and cannot focus his thoughts, causing us to abort our first Scrabble game. Sitting comfortably at the dining table is no longer possible for him, and so the game board balances precariously on his bed covers. The aged Scrabble set is nearly split in two pieces. A member of our family for over half a century, it sports thick and forceful pencil scribblings carved into its surface. *The handiwork, perhaps, of someone lifetimes ago who held her crayons too tightly?* That Dad can still strategize—forming multiple words, gaining points in several directions, and doubling or tripling his score by utilizing bonus squares—astounds me. His reprimand in our second game for my slowness in placing tiles on the board is well taken. My thoughts are not focused on brainy strategies but in one direction alone—his well-being.

"Sorry, Dad, I should be putting down words a lot faster."

Silence.

Little do I know this will be his last game.

"Linda, I don't want company today." All the same when Tommy, Liz, Perri, Tess, and Noah arrive, he rallies to greet everyone with tender fanfare. Like a lone bookend, I wrap my arms around my drawn-up knees and take my place on the corner of the bed once the family leaves to keep Dad company for a baseball game. His home team, the Chicago White Sox, just lost.

"It happens," he says faintly. "Linnie, will you sing for me?"

I tune my three-quarter-sized Martin, a six-string mahogany guitar that I grew up with. Much like a cat awaiting a good petting session, it sits easily on my lap with eagerness to be plucked and strummed.

"Okay," Dad interrupts me in the middle of the third song. "Stop. That's enough."

Aaron is uncomfortable yet he won't admit to being in pain. Even if he were hurting—and my instincts tell me he is—he wouldn't say. Dad is still being Dad. He doesn't want Vicodin, he won't ask for oxygen, he pales against the white sheets. The cards games are finished. The Scrabble has ended. Dad will be forever—Dad.

We may not always see the deeper lessons embedded within our life-tests. I'm seeing some of them now.

A ROCKY ROAD

*D*ear Sahaja,

It's good to hear from you, thank you for your loving concern. How are the hillsides north of Rome?

Only minutes ago, my father finally accepted the use of the oxygen machine. His fingers were literally turning blue. He faces each small loss of physical independence with unwillingness, sometimes with anger and impatience. And he's still walking, though with such shakiness that he may soon give that up too. That will be a big step for him as was no longer being able to drive about five months ago. Being bed-ridden isn't something my father will accept lightly!

I've been here for all of it, watching him give up one freedom after another with much difficulty and resistance. It makes me a thousand times more grateful for our spiritual path and inspires me to pray more deeply for my father.

Sometimes I feel such joy. Sometimes it feels like the tears will never stop. Someday I know I will be firmly anchored in *that joy, never to lose it.*

    In divine friendship,

    Lila

Dear Savitri,

    Well, either your prayers are very special, or I'm especially receptive to them because I'm feeling more rested and centered today.

    My father is failing. He's fighting his condition with tremendous will power. He won't, and can't, admit any weakness, which makes caring for him extremely difficult. He won't acknowledge that he can't walk to the bathroom alone anymore, instead falling back to sleep and sending me out the door.

    It appears that his way of exerting control over his life and securing that he hasn't lost that ability is to control me. He forbids me to talk to people for any length of time, either to visitors or to anyone on the telephone. I understand and am not bothered, but it's certainly awkward! Soon he may be withdrawn enough to not care about such details.

    Dad's road to Heaven is indeed a rocky one. Still, it's nearly over. I hope to be back at Ananda for this upcoming glorious anniversary weekend. My heart will know peace for the rest of my life that I've cared for my father in his last days.

    Our family is dealing reasonably well with the grief.

    It's hard to stay centered while being so thoroughly unrested and unwell, and at the same time holding a major care-taking position.

Thanks for listening. Please keep these details in confidence, which I appreciate. It helps to minimize the harsher elements.

Hope your perm turned out lovely as always.

Lila

Dear Lila,

My new perm is overly curly as usual, but will calm down in a few days or weeks. Glad the prayers seem to be helping. You and your father really need them, I can tell. I'll keep it all confidential, except to remind anyone who asks about you that you could use some increased prayer energy. Just think of what a great power-house of strength you're going to be when this is over and you've rested up a bit!

Call anytime. I am praying that you make it back up here for the big weekend, one way or another.

Savitri

Dear Savitri,

Dad is sleeping now, that deep sleep that may soon transition seamlessly into a coma. He's gone eight days without food, though the nutritional supplement drink is considered a meal. He had one of those yesterday.

I don't think he cares any more if I'm on the phone or not.

Watching my father in pain because he refuses to take any more medication than he's already on is one of the hardest parts about being here. He wants to be as conscious as possible and I support him in that. He says his pain level hovers around three out of ten—though I have reason to believe he's closer to ten.

As for me, I'm losing weight, sleeping badly, and experiencing sympathy pains in my back exactly where Dad is hurting. Mine is a muscle spasm while his is irritated nerves from a cancerous pancreas. Plus I've had three weeks of digestive problems—which never, ever happens—and two bad sore throats with fever, aches, and chills. I've been sick pretty much the whole time. Even so, I've managed to keep working out somewhat and eating okay. Not great, just okay. I'm even able to get some work done for my business plus Brenda, my directorial assistant (who's been ill herself), is doing well overseeing the office, which is a great blessing.

And yet behind all of this is the joy of the soul.

I'm going to prepare for a quick exit back to Ananda just in case. I'd stay for a day of the sitting shiva and then come home. I was even thinking to come back just for the big weekend if my father keeps lingering, but I'm not sure about that right now. We're taking this one day at a time.

So that's a little more news. Many thanks for your prayers,
Lila

Dearest Friend,

Thank you for returning my call from Los Angeles. I'm glad you let me know how your dad is doing. Just imagine the joy that the astral plane is having in receiving his soul back to its home! Now the human part of us is in sadness, but it's such a beautiful experience. So I'm going to be praying for you and for your dad that he may have a very uplifting transition.

God bless,

Bhaktimarg

In the Hands of Hashem

The moon hangs full in the sky, a lone Christmas tree ornament that God forgot to pack away after the holidays. It's been a wretched day for Dad. I feel to write very little. His moods shift to wide extremes and there's nothing about this time that I want to remember. He screeches at Moshe and family to leave. The noise, the visitors, all of it only seems to intensify his inner struggle. Everyone dear to my father's heart is now being forcibly removed.

Forest Lawn Cemetery a mere twenty minutes from Dad's condominium is where I turn for solace. Enshrined within its marbled halls are the mortal remains of an immortal master, my Guru. My favorite of his prayers is finely chiseled into the stone: "May Thy love shine forever on the sanctuary of my devotion and may I be able to awaken Thy love in all hearts." *Where else can one go for the strength to say good-bye to a beloved parent?* No place, no person, no thing can comfort me. Seated in the mausoleum in a meditative pose, I draw God's unbroken grace into my broken yet persevering spirit. If my soul had knees, they would be worn with calluses by now from kneeling incessantly in prayer.

The hospice nurse will arrive soon at the shrine of Dad's home, and then we'll know how to proceed. It's time for my brothers to step forward to care for him.

It is time for me to leave.

Nurse Nan like many hospice workers has lost close relatives to cancer. She visits from 10:30 to midnight and Dad responds well to her soft voice and gentle ways. Everything about her is comforting. Her eyes shine with compassion chiseled from assisting many people in their transition from this world to the next—some with reticence, some with anger, some with grace.

Aaron: "I'm ready to die. It's not easy to die. I'm very proud of what I've built." His last sentence is so faint that I must repeat it for her.

Nan: "Is four out of ten your acceptable level of pain?" This is the first I've heard of an elevated pain level. He's never mentioned higher than three.

Aaron: "I'll be okay. What color are your eyes?"

Nan: "They're dark brown. Is there any way I can make the pain better?"

Aaron: "It doesn't really matter. How can you tell when somebody is dying?"

Nan: "When they're not responsive or talking, when there's no stimulation from touch or noise." After a slight pause she says tenderly, "I can tell you're in pain."

Aaron: "Hold my hand. You have nice warm hands. Have you

met my children? I have five children. This is my oldest. My only daughter. God gave her to me."

Nan: "I can see why you're so proud. You have good reason to be."

Aaron: "My boys. I'm so proud of all my boys. And my girl. My treasure. . ." His voice trails into a light, vaporized sigh.

Once Dad dozes off, Nan and I retire to the living room to speak privately.

"Your father's behavior and body language show that he's scared out of his wits." Nan folds her hands, one on top of the other, like embroidered linen napkins. "His pain level may be much higher than he's telling you, Linda. You need to ask him to accept your help. He needs you. But his pride won't let him ask you for anything. He sees that as a sign of infirmity. Your Dad is afraid of losing himself. You can help him with that by being there for him just as you always have. Dying people always want someone there because of the fear. They feel abandoned but a bother at the same time."

"Thanks, Nan, you've been a great help. It's late now and I'm seriously over-tired."

"Don't worry, I'll stay while you rest."

"Actually, I'm not comfortable with that idea. Would you mind leaving?"

The mild-mannered nurse harbors a will of steel that she wields to override my request that she leave now, and our encounter becomes a dual between her interpretation of my needs and my own understanding of them. This clash of intentions is a little rough for me to manage, especially at such a fragile time. Nurse-schmurse. *Caretaking the caregiver?*

I am becoming acutely aware that my father's soul is pushing me away. He leaves me no choice but to go. As close as we were, Mom needed the psychic perimeters of my absence from Los Angles in order to move on, and the same appears true for Dad. Tomorrow I will return home. *How can he leave this world while receiving the ministrations of his daughter? And still wanting to care for his little girl?* It's time for my brothers to wrap their auras around him.

All five of us kids agree on a plan.

"You come back on Sunday, Sis, ya hear? That's only three days from now." Phil commands the football huddle of siblings with a comforting decisiveness.

"What's taking so long?"

"What do you mean, Dad?"

He will not or cannot reply.

The mid-afternoon flight means a quick exit deliberately planned. Like my Jewish ancestors before me, my innate sense of competition drives me to excel in the simple art of travel preparation, as though I've entered a suitcase-packing competition with the goal to win and not merely tie for first place. I execute the sloppiest packing job ever. Clothing and toiletries are flung into the empty cavern of my stunned suitcase.

This game serves its purpose well—to distract me from what I'm about to do. The time has come to say good-bye to my father.

The Mary Poppins of hospice social workers appears, landing like a fictional character on the doorstep as if from everywhere and nowhere. Before she speaks a word, I already know that whatever she says will be perfectly right, divinely guided, exactly what I need to hear. These days with Dad have forcibly pried me from my normal consciousness into an altered state where life is anything but real. It reads like fiction. Nothing makes sense. Everything feels raw, scattered, free-falling—or as yogic teachings explain when one makes an intense effort over time in his spiritual practices, effortlessly liberating.

"It's common for a dying person," the hospice worker explains, "to openly confide in caregivers other than their immediate family. Your father doesn't want to show any of you that he's dependent or vulnerable."

With a soft knock on the front door resembling the sweep of a squirrel's tail against an oak tree, Moshe, Bracha, and Chana arrive. First Chana leaves in tears, then Jackie Sunshine.

But it's on me, Dad's primary caregiver and the sole child of five whom he could never control, upon whom he unleashes the full force of his wrath over the loss of his life. The psychic tissues in my body feel as though they're being torn apart and my muscles, both large and small, seem stretched beyond their normal limberness. Whether the blood is flowing freely in my veins or in the correct amounts and directions, I cannot tell—or if it's flowing at all. As much as I'm able to understand and impersonalize Dad's behavior at this stage of his dying process, my very bones feel shattered. All I know is that I'm returning to my community for a weekend of celebration with my life, goals, and dreams intact after having done everything I can for my beloved outrageous father—and that my prayers for him will continue.

My ministrations here are finished. Dad is in the hands of Hashem.

Dearest Jackie and Tommy,

Still waiting to hear back about tonight's caregiver, either Moshe or Phil, looks like Moshe.

You know, it would be wonderful if you both stopped in tonight even briefly. Dad's mostly sleeping in a deeper way now. For you to come by would be a great comfort to him.

Love having you as my brothers,

Favorite Sis forever

Divine grace and my spiritual training are bolstering me to endure this grievous time. The *Bhagavad Gita* puts it well, saying, "Where there is *dharma*"—meaning righteous action—"there is victory." *And joy*. The strength I've gained through my years of spiritual practices has allowed me to care for Dad. Aaron hasn't been an easy father, nor is it easy to lose him. I have shed many tears, and my sense of loss is colossal. Yet no suffering is senseless or without purpose, as I have come to understand, while he soldiers on with the inner work of his own spiritual journey.

A wispy trail of unfinished dreams is slipping through my fingers, never to see fruition. In part I'm mourning the finality of losing forever the *possibility* of ever having the father I wanted; the charmed childhood as "Daddy's little girl" without ambiguity or ambivalence; and the chance to reconcile the challenging pattern of a paternal love that has been in portions both lavished and withheld.

We all want death to happen a certain way, though it rarely goes the way we think it will.

Several years ago, the national news reported a skydiving mishap. The diver's parachute failed to deploy in a free fall. Finally the reserve chute opened seven hundred feet from the ground only to malfunction. She hit the ground at eighty miles an hour, shattering half her body and knocking the fillings from her teeth. Landing on a red anthill did little to break her fall. To compound the diver's agony, the agitated ants stung her over two hundred times. With timely irony, they probably saved her life! The doctors concurred that the multiple stings shocked her heart enough to keep it beating.

"All is grace," said the young saint Therese, cloistered for most of her short life as a Carmelite nun in Lisieux, France.

I can't say that having Aaron as my father rivals freefalling from the sky into a pile of red ants! Had my relationship with him been perfect, I probably wouldn't have developed the fortitude to leave the lifestyle into which I'd been born for the life I was born to live.

I would have married the doctor, the lawyer, or the rabbi. *All is grace.* Indeed.

With this insight comes the realization that nothing remains to resolve with my father. The knowing that Aaron played his role to perfection gives me peace. It must be grace that allows me to grasp this certainty before he passes away, far away from the remainder of my life. Dad made me tough, independent, determined, and more. He never let me win at checkers. He never played easy with me. In this moment, I feel only gratitude for him—*exactly as he is and just as he was—and how it has brought me to where I am now.*

The time has come to say good-bye to my father. In leaving him I feel like that skydiver in a freefall, not knowing how the landing will fare. Either I'll hit the ground half-shattered, or like a butterfly with fiercely strong wings, land ever so lightly.

My father asks for the longest backrub ever, not wanting me to stop. I kiss him and leave the room to finish packing, then return to kiss him once more. *Don't make a scene. Don't fall apart. Do not make this any harder for either of you than it already is.* Dad takes my hand, gripping it firmly like a tennis racket. Not comfortably, not gracefully, but very tightly.

"I'll never forget you, Linda." *Silence.*

Time to leave Los Angeles for my home. *Home? Where and what is home?*

Home is my heart's land, home's where I am.
Nothing can dim the light of my soul.
Home is forever, home is today.
Home's a heart that is whole.[10]

Tommy's voicemail tells me that everything is fine, he and Jackie visited Dad. "Last night Dad said he's been thinking a lot about Mom. He's happier that you've gone back home for three days and will be returning on Sunday to resume caring for him. He misses you quite a bit and he's looking forward to your return to care for him."

That's Dad, forever watchful of his kids.

Once back in my familiar world in the foothills that seems strangely unfamiliar, sister-in-law Patty phones. "Your agenda is so loving and admirable, Linda. This is the hardest time for a family. My husband is trying to be a doctor to his own father.

"What you're doing is amazing. The humanity and love are there, and you can sleep at night knowing you've done the right thing." My response is an exhalation of stillness, weariness, resolution. "Look, Linda. You took on something bigger than life and death that no one human being can do. I'm fearful of dying because I have nothing to grab onto, nothing to believe in. And that makes it scary. I think it will be easier for you when your time comes."

"How are you, Dad?"

"Not so good." The shadow of his voice on the phone is thin, faint, ethereal. "I'm so glad you called. I love you, Dolly. I love you. Bye."

Moshe tells me, putting another call on hold, "In my two days with Dad—from Thursday when you left, Sis, until today—I walked Dad to the bathroom many times. He needed some help getting up, but he insisted on walking by himself."

Our parent has survived this ordeal without becoming bed-ridden. He has held fast to his independence. And most importantly, death would soon fail to pry his dignity from his fierce grasp.

Home is forever, home is today. Home's a heart that is whole.

Torn Black Velvet

Sunday, September 14, 2008, 2:45 a.m.

I reach for the landline after four rings, fumbling in the silent darkness of my country abode. Never in all these months on my trips home have I slept with the telephone plugged in, a mere arm's reach from the bed on the nightstand.

It's Phil, crying and unable to speak. Finally he says, "Dad's in a peaceful place now."

"Oh, Philly." I call my-brother-the-doctor by Mom's nickname for him.

"Dad had a very peaceful expression on his face. He was just holding on. Every breath was labored. He was struggling. He went out with dignity. I walked in to check in on him at 11 last night, and that was our last conversation."

After a long battle in this world, Dad finally landed in Heaven.

Phil recounted the final moments. Dressed only in his boxer shorts, he walked into the bedroom. "Dad gave me a real big smile. Why he smiled like that, Sis, I don't know. Maybe I looked ridiculous. Maybe he was just real happy to see me. 'Dad, I'm going to bed,' I told him. 'You need me, you give a yell, I'll come.'"

Shortly after, Phil heard commotion. "I was going to get up and didn't. I think I saw a light, I don't know, he may have gotten up. Dad must have gotten himself out of bed, turned on the bathroom light, and walked into my room. Apparently he decided not to wake me up. All this moving about from a man who'd been starving and dehydrated for two weeks!"

Of two possible reasons Dad's his actions, one is that he went to Phil for help knowing his heart was failing—a condition for which he had been hospitalized a year earlier. Had that been so, he easily could have awakened Phil. The other reason? *To see his firstborn son one last time.*

"Then he walked back to his room and sat down on the floor beside his bed. At 2:15 a.m. it was very still, though his respirations earlier were labored.

"I walked in and saw Dad was gone. He'd left us."

Phil's medical intuition had guided him to check in on Dad moments after his passing. Phil found him sitting on the floor of the bedroom, propped up against the side of the bed with his feet facing the bathroom. His legs were crossed at the ankles. He was leaning heavily on his fists, his head slumped over.

"It was very clear by his posture that he hadn't simply fallen. Linda, it was so nice to come into the room and see Dad at peace. He didn't want to die in bed. The lingering anger during his last days showed us how much he wanted to remain in complete control of his life. We couldn't have done more to make it better for him, Sis. We gave him his dignity—no VA Hospital, no IVs. He went out very nicely. I was trying to feel if he was still there, I don't know how long it takes. I'm sure he *was* there for a while, hovering. I felt it was important for me to stay close to him for that time."

Dad's eyes were closed by his tearful son who for a time sat with him and held his hand. Phil called the mortuary, then Patty, me, the brothers—in order of descending age as was our family tradition. He was unable to reach Jackie so Tommy drove the fifteen minutes from Pacific Palisades to Santa Monica. Jackie took the news well.

Hospice arrived at 4 a.m. "Congestive heart failure," Phil wrote as the cause-of-death on the death certificate. Had he not been the attending physician as well as "the attending son"—which in itself was a miracle of sorts—the lengthy paperwork most likely would have delayed the funeral.

"I had a feeling I'd be with Dad at the end," Phil said resolutely. Just like his father, he took charge of the situation with great will power.

Phil can fix anything.

I've always thought people die exactly as they live. As conflicted as human beings are, we're also surprisingly consistent. Dad lived on his own terms and he died the same way. He beat this disease. No way was he going to let the cancer take his life. He died of an overtaxed heart.

Home is my heart's land, home's where I am. Nothing can dim the light of my soul.

Hastily packed in my carry-on luggage is a black velvet blouse, its nap shifting and shimmering in diverse light and shade, much like the coat of a wild animal in the prime of his life. I will wear this outfit every day in the week ahead for *kariya*, the Jewish rending of clothing at a funeral service. A practice with a dual meaning, it depicts the grief of the mourner and also signifies that it is only "the clothing of the soul" that is torn away from the deceased while the soul itself lives on forever.

News reaches me at 8:30 a.m. of the 2 p.m. funeral. This afternoon? *Ya gotta be kidding me.* "But I'm sitting at home in my pajamas!" as Noah would say. I phone in the reservation en route to the Sacramento airport. A two-hour drive to the departure gate, an hour's wait to board, and a one-hour flight followed by an hour-long drive to the cemetery. Here I sit, awaiting a plane back to Los Angeles exactly three days after telling Dad I'd see him again—in three days.

The caretaking is finished. I'm going to my father's funeral.

I recline in a daze at the airport restaurant like a guest at the Passover table, expressing my inner freedom by leaning against a long wall of windows overlooking a row of docked airplanes. Numbly I go through the motions of eating a bowl of vegetarian pea soup, furtively swallowing giant spoonfuls of the thick green liquid. Its amorphous nature reminds me of the tofu at Bamboo with Dad—sweet and sour, so like this transitory moment of relief and emptiness.

Is it my imagination, or did the chef forget to add flavor the recipe? Ree-ally, you call this a *soup* spoon? It's gigantic. *Who in their right mind would make a spoon so large?* This isn't dinnerware, it's a ladle. Ladle-schmadle. What are they, nuts?

The waitress is harried though kindly as if to make amends for the oversized eating utensil. I thank her by name for bringing the check just as my father would have done. Tommy rings my cell phone. We converse about how beautifully scripted Dad's passing was. "Sis, ya know I heard somewhere," he says in a calm but tired voice, "that a parent's last lesson to his children is how he leaves this world. Dad was a glowing example of that wisdom."

"You got *that* right." Spoken just like him—same words, same tone of voice.

"Until the end he modeled courage, dignity, grace, and strength of will for all his kids, don't you think, Sis? Hey, Sis. Are you still there?"

"Yes, baby brother, caught every word." I dab a sliver of carrot from my mouth with a corner of my napkin. The oversized polyester cloth reminds me of the sheets on Dad's foldout sofa. "But mostly it's all about love. Tommy Boy, did I ever tell you what my girlfriend once said, the one who lost both her parents? 'The hardest part is feeling like no one knows me.' That didn't make any sense to me until now. Tell me, do you feel like an orphan?"

"Yeah. Linda, we're fresh out of parents."

My father is such a large part of my life that I'm clueless about how to separate us.

How fitting to be dressed in black, as though all the color has drained from my life. The tennis shoes Dad bought for me on one of our shopping trips hasten my steps through the Burbank Airport, and the thick cotton socks he fished out of Mom's dresser drawer keep my feet warm in the air-conditioned terminal. "Here, take them," he told me, stuffing the socks unceremoniously into my hands, "you'll wear them in the best of health." *Yes, father mine, on the day we celebrate your freedom from this world.* Dressed so slipshod yet so practical, I jog past the rows of boarding gates to my left and right and then out the exit door as though running through someone else's dream, with no checked luggage to slow my progress to the funeral site. My carryon suitcase is as much of a joke as Dad's guest bed. It seems to have a mind of its own, the wheels digging in their heels like an errant child being coaxed from a toy store.

The plane docks twenty-five minutes late. Jackson, accessorized in kindliness tinted with grief, retrieves me at the airport, eliminating the further delay of standing in a taxi queue and ensuring my arrival at the cemetery exactly one minute before the ceremony begins. Another miracle on this day I will remember always. *Linda, I will never forget you.* My-brother-the-rabbi is quietly grateful to see his sister. True, the family would have waited for me, but 2 p.m. today is the only time slot available for the funeral service. Jewish orthodoxy counsels the interment of the deceased as quickly as possible. My father's body is buried half a day after his passing.

We did it, Dad. You and me, we're a team. We got you to Heaven.

There is little to say about the funeral. We all pass through it with hushed emotions.

Nothing seems real. Dad, *gone*? I manage my way through it by asking God to hold my hand. Not comfortably, not gracefully, but very tightly. These words—savored from the Old Testament like droplets of wine from a goblet at the Sabbath table—give me sustenance:

I will lift up mine eyes unto the hills,
From whence cometh my help.
My help cometh from the Lord,
Who made the heavens and the earth.

The glorious afternoon is made bright by a light deeper than the sun. Loved ones hover silently in the afternoon heat. The grass at my father's gravesite is exquisitely green, covering the hillside in a radiant sea of life force. *Has grass ever been so brilliantly colored?* The funeral seems dreamlike from beginning to end, fashioned like the song from a Jewish play, "laden with happiness and tears."

My four brothers stand tall in their suits and *yamulkes*. So fine, so handsome. How proud I am of them all! Just as I'm sure Dad is. Scattered about everywhere across the life-affirming landscape are my father's children and their children. Friends, neighbors, and those who have come to honor him gather round. The rabbi asks permission to tear the shirts of Aaron's five children—a gesture signifying that our hearts too are torn and we are in mourning.

With such delicate graciousness, he approaches Aaron's daughter at the last. Who he is, I don't know but the sacred ritual of *kariya* binds us together in a shared humanity. Here stands a man of delicate but firm nature deeply rooted in Judaic tradition—one who sips the scriptures with reverence. *But a rabbi stepping forward to tear my shirt at my father's funeral?* How can this be happening? It's time for Dad's breakfast and a few more stories! He beat me last time in cards and almost always at Scrabble and checkers, so I must try harder to win our next game. My father modeled for me how to win, or to die trying. Death-schmeath, it's just another game. He struggled his way out of material poverty, and he taught me, spiritually, to do the same.

At Dad's funeral, time isn't merely standing still as the poets are wont to say. It races forwards and backwards and sideways in the spirit of the rain on the Umbrian hills, all out of rhythm with itself. How is this day even possible?

Oh. Because I'm dreaming. Because life is a dream. *And yes, in the dream this day is more than possible.*

I sit in the front row shaded by a canopy before the gravesite, watching my father's burial. Brother Moshe glances over at me. "You looked like a queen, Sis," he tells me later, perhaps intuiting my simple prayer: *take my hand, take my hand.* Floating some-where outside myself, I look on as the coffin—a plain pine box as prescribed by orthodox law—is lowered into the ground. My brothers do not participate in this part of the ceremony. Instead other menfolk who knew and loved my father shovel dirt onto the casket, a heartfelt custom signifying the stepping forward of the Jewish community to comfort their bereaved.

The casket is covered all the same, just as my father once requested. His burial plot rests beside my mother's atop a hill-side. A silly, senseless thought comes to me, the youthful musing of a parentless child: *Wait a minute, something is amiss. Dad always slept on the other side of Mom.*

You got that right.

We walk back from the gravesite, a speechless sea of mourners in black suits, black dresses, black hats, to wash our hands at the curbside spigot. The Jewish tradition of hand-washing symboliz-es our transition from what comes before to what transpires after.

Eternally Yours — All Aboard!

August 31, 1949
Hello, My Love:

Your voice is like a bubbling spring, do you mind if I drink from your banks more often? My love for you increases and grows more tender as the days go by. How I wish they passed sooner, so that the beautiful lady who has been my dream will become my reality.

A man can realize nothing greater than the materialization of all that he has longed for and soon, my darling, you will be mine. Hope this letter reaches you before I do, so that I may repeat my love for you again and again. Enough to say I'll love and cherish you through all of our years on earth and in Heaven?

A girl just called to ask me for a date, and I told her she would have to ask my wife. Only kidding, Baby. There's just one place for me—Detroit—near you.

My thoughts have wandered into the future, and I'm wondering how my trip to Detroit is going to turn out. With you in my presence, life is complete, with you beside me everything is sweet, with you beside me I'll brave the ice and sleet, with you beside me I'll withstand the rain and heat. Next trip around this world leaving in fifteen minutes. All aboard!

Frank and Mick went to a dance downtown, and Mom is busy writing up postal cards for her auxiliary. She will write you one day this week, I promise. Enclosed you'll find our new circular. It looks very good to me. All comments accepted. As I write this letter the room is filled with soft symphonic music. Very conducive to good thought, eh what?

Yesterday I visited Ver and Vern. Their baby girl is so wonderful.

Mom made my favorite dish for lunch and supper tonight. My appetite has greatly increased. I told Mom to see that the boys get more to eat, for we will all need as much energy as possible the next few months.

I closed my eyes in order to get a clearer picture of you just then. My Baby is so beautiful. I love you, for you are mine, and I am yours. Forever.

Aaron

P.S. Love to all from all!

Putting the Ball Away

On the night of his passing, I dreamed about Dad. I heard him as though he was standing next to me.

With full voice he said: "I enjoyed being your father."

"Heya, Sis," Tommy says, "the *minyan* of ten Jewish men was hard to gather last night, though we ended up with fifteen. That's five more than the minimum needed to say *Kaddish*. There just wasn't enough time for people to know. Tonight will be packed."

My bigger-than-life father has become bigger than death.

"Thanks for telling me, Tommy Boy. You know, I'm on the outskirts of these 'men ceremonies.'"

At tonight's *shiva*, the last night before I return home, my brothers and other loved ones speak about Dad. The siblings take turns shifting their legs on the cushion-less chairs and sofas. We are not only mourning the loss of our father but also of certain comforts as part of this weeklong custom, the word *shiva* itself meaning *seven*. In Hindu text the Lord Shiva is personified as the destroyer of delusion and hence the death of all that isn't real—a comment on the similarity of these concepts from two God-oriented paths and how they embrace the underlying truths of both religions.

The house lamps shed a respectful lighting on the steady trickle of visitors who tread softly, encouraging immediate-family mourners to initiate conversations. Some people bring food that earns them a *mitzvah*. Others fill their plates. According to custom, we do not exchange greetings with arriving guests nor do we acknowledge their departure. Those who leave recite to us, "May God comfort you among the other mourners of Zion and Jerusalem."

Just imagine the joy that the astral plane is having in receiving your father's soul back to his home! The human part of us is in sadness but it's such a beautiful experience. My friend's sentiments resonate with the brilliance that shines in my brothers' eyes. We have just offered our second parent to higher realms. It seems to us that Mom and Dad in some tangible way were the umbilical cords that tied us, if not to this world, then to how it defines us.

Within the walls of Moshe's home, an aura of hushed anticipation surrounds the mystery of death. Dad is now free and so are his five children.

"He never had difficulty making a decision and he always stuck by it," Phil says.

The words of Aaron's oldest son float through the silent room of a house built in the days of silent films. Its wrought iron balustrades, hardwood floors, and stained glass windows fortify our souls. The aged musical instrument of Moshe's home in the heart of orthodox Los Angeles has absorbed the notes played upon it. In this house, children have grown into adulthood while the cycles of holidays—ruled by the moon on the Jewish calendar—spun like festive Chanukah dreidels. This dwelling has registered the lives of its occupants in its etheric guestbook. In Moshe's neighborhood, only Gentiles drive on the Sabbath. Otherwise the streets are abandoned weekly for that one sacred day—motionless except for the men and women dressed in black, making their way on foot to temple for prayer.

Dad's loved ones sit in the sunken living room where our spirits rise in a river mist above our saddened joy—the same room where a year shy of a week ago we gathered to celebrate his eightieth birthday. Phil leans forward on the unfriendly couch, resting his fork on a plate of bagels, lox, and potato salad.

"Dad was never wishy-washy whether he was right or wrong. He had an amazing decision-making power. If you were right, he backed you. If you were wrong, he told you so. I got my decisiveness from Dad."

In response to his older brother's insights, Jack speaks next. "Dad was a very intense person, a very strong person." The day-old stubble on my brother's chin will not see a razor for another six days, a custom acknowledging the shift of focus from ourselves to our father's soul. According to *shiva* traditions, cloths cover every mirror in Moshe's house.

"When Dad first began as a salesman," Moshe says, "he found that the receptionists in the doctors' offices tended to put him off. Always they were telling him he might have to wait an hour or two to maybe even *see* the doctor? Not what you'd call a very viable way for a man with a large family to make a living!" Moshe leans back in the upright armchair, tapping his eyebrows with his fingers, a gesture perhaps intended to stimulate his brain cells—the same fingers that have turned voluminous pages of scripture in reverent study of Jewish law.

"Dad's superiors suggested that he drop an ash tray on the waiting room floor and then ask for a broom in hopes of—ya never know—running into the doctor. Oh *no-o*, he didn't like that idea at all! Instead he developed his people skills to a level that brought him tremendous success in connecting with the doctors and receptionists as well as a remarkable level of sales."

Tommy sighs. Speaking eloquently in a court of law comes easily to him. His ongoing joke is how as a kid he honed his winning skills in the art of argument within the chambers of the family home. In that same refinement of verbal talent, he begins.

"Dad loved to talk to people. But he wasn't the type of person who had a hard time with silence. He was interested in people and always wanted to get to know them. Dad talked with a purpose. It was something beautiful about him.

"He was all about not being too serious and finding the positives in everything. His glass was never half empty. It was always completely full, he always gave a positive spin."

Brothers mine: Dad would be so proud of you.

Hi Linda,

I realized tonight that I don't have your address! I'd like to have that. So please e-mail me your home address. I hope you're holding up all right. It was very nice at tonight's shiva. I didn't know if I should say anything about your dad, so I kept quiet. I think the talks are supposed to come from his children.

Right?

Everywhere I go, I see your dad. What I mean is, I reached into a drawer and there was the tape measure your dad gave me. Then there's that great scissors he bought for me too! He left such a void in my life, and I miss him terribly.

Zeke said I should always have flowers. He used to buy me flowers quite often. He was such a sweet and thoughtful man, Linda, and I loved him with all my heart and soul. I'll never forget him. I'll carry him in my heart, just like I know you will too.

See you tomorrow evening. What time did you say you planned on getting there? I'm tiring out, what with working all day and running around at night. Tomorrow might be my last night for going to shiva. I don't think anyone will think badly of me, do you?

Love,

Jackie Sunshine

Dearest Jackson,

Do you know how precious you are to everyone who knows you?

We're all a little worried about you right now because your heart is so tender and this is such a great loss for you. Oh, I'm so sorry. Jackson, you are being a real trooper. I know Dad is proud of you for your strength and for how well you are bearing his passing to Heaven. You touched him so deeply in ways that no one else ever has. He said this time and time again.

You know, I'm a novice at the shiva *rules too. It might be better to ask Moshe about sharing some words. We're all taking our leads from him. Personally, I think it's a great idea.*

After tonight's prayers ended, the talk got very joyful in remembrance of Dad. My brothers spoke and I asked Moshe if I was allowed to speak a little as well. He gave me a thumbs up. I shared something identical to what you wrote: that now Dad lives in our hearts and how I see him in each of my brothers.

A woman who was there—I forget her name, the lovely lady who brought the kosher chocolate cake—asked Moshe if the five of us were being appropriate because we were so unabashedly joyful in our stories of Dad. She acted shocked by our behavior. Moshe said it was fine and no rules were being broken.

Dearest Jackie, it's so beautiful of you to say that you see my father everywhere. It sounds like your love for him is expanding even in his absence. How rare and precious when love continues to grow after the beloved passes—a testimony to the purity of your love for him.

We all want you to know how much you have given to Dad. I know you already understand that love is never lost, and that surely he is receiving your love even now in Heaven.

We're all grateful for whatever time you are able to attend. No one will think badly of you! Tommy says we'll get there slightly earlier tomorrow than today. So, maybe 4:30 or 5-ish? I hope you can arrive early too so we can have more time together. I look forward to seeing you and meeting your cousin.

Jackie, if my father said you should always have flowers, then you should always have flowers. Every bouquet can be an expression of his love for you, a love that will live through eternity.

Much love,

Linda

The *shiva* stories continue. Dad comes to life in our memories of him. He sits beside us on the sofas, stripped of their comfort in his honor. He whispers between our thoughts and pauses within our breaths.

Tommy's friend Josh clears his throat. "I got to know Zeke and then saw him briefly as a patient. When you think about who a person is, his legacy is so important. And you see sitting here five children, each of whom is very different from the others. One thing they have that is so apparent is a deep love. The legacy that will come from this depth of devotion is what is passed down to his grandchildren. Because Zeke was such a great person, I think more than anything else the love will speak for itself."

"Your dad reminds me of my dad." Josh's wife Melanie sips her soda to the clink of ice cubes and the fizz of carbonation. "He made you feel so comfortable from the first time you met him. For me, this was at Liz and Tom's wedding. The guy grabbed me and danced with me He absolutely loved life! And the way your dad exited this world with such incredible dignity—it was a privilege to know him.

"I hope my kids feel the same way about me as all five of you feel about your dad."

"The Talmud says that it was a blessing unto Jacob," my-brother-the-rabbi adds, "this custom that comes from saying 'bless you' when you sneeze. It used to be that a person would sneeze and then die. Jacob prayed to God that people should get sick before dying because someone who starts sneezing and then just dies— it doesn't allow for wrapping up loose ends. The first mention of old age is by Abraham. And he was *old*, I'm *tellink* you. Jacob became ill, and his sons called to receive the blessings. According to the scriptures, Jacob was the first person to get ill before he died. This was God's decision. Jacob prayed to God that there should be illness so that people wouldn't just die without any warning.

"It would have been difficult for our family if Dad had died suddenly. He chose not to take pain medication. The nurse said on a scale of one to ten, his pain level was close to ten, even though he said it was only a three. Having an illness before passing is a response to Jacob's prayer.

"This was the *mitzvah* of Dad's illness. It gave us all time for closure, and even more importantly to express the deeper love between us."

The mood begins to lighten as our stories about Dad quicken like a séance where the dead are mythically coaxed back to life. "Two days before he passed Dad asked, 'Who am I?' This is talked about in the Torah. It happens when a soul faces God and asks this deep question."

"One day, Dad drove me to school to carry my art assignment to class," I hear myself saying. I shift my weight on the sofa before realizing a more comfortable position won't be possible. "It was my junior year in high school, and my project was an oversized hooked rug. Dad followed me down the hall. All the kids were staring at me, and then back at him. I kept wondering, *what's going on?* When I finally turned around to see what they were looking at, there was Dad, dancing like Gene Kelly! The rolled-up rug was slung over his shoulder, and he had a big grin on his face. Life was a musical comedy to Dad. And he had no problem embarrassing the heck out of me."

"Uncle Aar was a great guy." Cousin Martin rises to leave. "When I close my eyes and see his face, I see a beguiling smile. It was always there. Whenever I met Uncle Aar, his face would light up. He always made you feel welcome and at home. He was big *kibbutzer*, a great kidder. I don't recall any specific jokes, but he would make light of things and he was never mean, always light-hearted. What bothered me as a kid was his off-putting cigars. I thought, 'Oh, that stinks!'

"I love you all."

Next an elderly gentleman rises from his chair to speak—an accomplished dermatologist, Moshe tells us later. "Your father won't have to reincarnate. He made people comfortable. This is a great loss to all who knew him, especially you four sons and daughter."

"We're talking about how every person Dad met was an opportunity to help someone, to give away some of his happiness," Moshe says.

Each shared vignette raises the joy level in the room as our reminiscences about Aaron gather momentum and flow more freely. The joy of honoring Dad's *shiva* animates Moshe Dovid, every new story a Hebrew song at a family gathering. Like the blessed message of so many Jewish holidays, our bereavement is infused with a wellspring of celebration: *We fought. We won. Let's eat.*

Moshe continues. "Dad's life was quite legendary. He got laid off from the pharmaceutical company, Lincoln Laboratories, and ended up in surgical supplies. He worked on his relationships with the nurses and secretaries. *Oy*, he became so good at finding out about people, taking a profound interest in them. His skills were growing every day. At eighty years old, he was taken in the prime of his life like Thurman Munson, the all-star catcher for the Yankees who was killed in a plane crash at thirty-two years of age in his athletic prime. Dad was still growing.

"At a restaurant Dad wouldn't order until he knew the name of the waitress. It was ree-ally something to see."

"Oh, Dad would be more embarrassing than *that*!" Jackie interjects. "'Do you dance? Do you sing?' His waitress knew it would be fun to wait on his table. Once in a restaurant at Lake Michigan, he stole a coin from a kid who was about to drop it in a juke box. 'You know what?' Dad asked the boy. 'I'll sing any song you want if you give me that nickel!'"

"Ya had ta see it!" Moshe slaps his knee in the manner of a kid highlighting the punchline of his own joke. "Such an enthusiasm and passionate love of life he had! It made you have a fun time too."

"We wrote *I Love Lucy,*" David Israel says. "Not really, just kidding." He and Joel Cohen, television script writers, squeeze together on the smallest sofa in the living-room-turned-amphitheater.

"I knew your dad through Tom and the Three Musketeers," Joel teases my brothers.

David gazes above the sea of faces. "What we liked about your dad?" he asks, as if repeating a question that was already asked. "Your father was warm, friendly, competitive. The room lit up every time I saw him smile. He had a great sense of humor." David's lightness of spirit brings levity to an already buoyant atmosphere, especially considering that we were honoring the custom of sitting *shiva*. "I didn't like him very much. I don't like Tom, I like the other children. I will forever be able to hear your dad singing, 'Had-Gad-Yah.' He was always welcome at our house for *Seders*, breakfast, and *Shabbat*. We would battle over which was the right way to sing, and Zeke always sang louder.

"I loved his storytelling. He talked about the old days. Even a month ago, Zeke was sensational. I always asked him questions —you didn't have to say a lot to get him going! He told a story about the first time he met your mother, and he went on with *elan*. I would watch him fill up with life. It was amazing. It's like he was there yesterday, sharing the details and the jokes. *Your father was remarkable*. I went from knowing him through Tom-down-the-block to where I always felt I didn't need you guys to have Zeke. I felt he was my friend. We connected and I loved him.

"My first sense now is how badly I feel for you guys because you lost this tremendous life force. Then I get selfish and start missing Zeke for my own sake. Whether it's the White Sox, or tennis, or poker—he had a wealth of knowledge. He was funny. He'd always go back to whatever was funny. I felt like I was just talking to a friend, he was so easy to talk to."

Moshe Dovid has hosted many Sabbaths and holidays over the years but never his own father's *shiva*. He moderates the evening well—acknowledging people's strengths and talents, always directing the focus back to Hashem. "Dad had a reverence for Judaism and that Jewish law was exactly the way to conduct one's life.

"I decided in high school to go to Yeshiva. 'How would you feel if I left?' I asked Dad. I was sixteen years old at the time. 'I'd be very proud,' Dad said without batting an eye. Later he tells me—and I'm not kidding, 'You should have taken some of your brothers with you.'

"I said a special prayer with Dad before he passed. In those prayers the person says, 'May my death be an atonement for anything I've done wrong.'"

I remembered that visit a mere couple of weeks ago. Withdrawing to the living room, I left the father and his son alone in the bedroom-shrine for privacy, sensing strongly that something sacred was transpiring.

"Dad didn't want to communicate with anyone in the last days of his life," Moshe went on. "The last words he asked me were, 'Who am I?' This is written in the scriptures.

"When Phil went into the room a few hours after I left, Dad was sitting on the floor with his legs crossed toward the door. He positioned himself this way in a posture of prayer instead of having other people do it for him. What was the significance of Dad's question? The idea is that a person says a prayer in order not to forget his own name and then gets called before the Heavenly court. The soul stands before the Creator and is asked to step forward. This is the soul's first experience in front of God. And then to find that Dad placed himself on the floor, a humble preparation for meeting the Creator . . .

"Dad told me a couple times during *Shabbos*, 'I am dying.' You're more a soul than a body at that point, so you don't relate to people in a physical milieu. It was frustrating," Moshe concludes, "because he made it clear that he didn't want to talk to me anymore."

Every room in Moshe's home is filled with *Nichum Aveilim,* the compassionate act of those who visit a *shiva* house to comfort the bereaved and let them know they are not alone. Homemade dishes of kosher delicacies are being eagerly eaten and summarily replaced. People chat freely in groups around the food table, while from the living room where my brothers and I sit, stories about Dad pour forth like *kiddush* wine.

"One night," Chana says, "me and Sara had dinner in The Valley with Zayde. We accidentally, like, spilled a glass of water all over him! We, like, felt so terrible and he was all, like, 'Thank you, I was feeling so warm!'"

"Zayde loved to dance," Sara adds, animated with vivacity. "Like, any time there was music he would, like, sing and dance with such spontaneity."

Phil withdraws into the *shiva* sofa. The saga of the 1947 softball game is begging to be narrated. "Dad told his brother Mickey this story every time he talked to him. Zeke was called in as a pitcher against a team of men of color. He was on a good team, but the other team was better. You know in those days, it was common for amateur baseball teams to play teams of color. That was after the highly successful Negro Leagues barnstorming tours of the 1930s and 40s. Dad was asked, 'Can you pitch? We're going to get killed.' *Oy*, he got destroyed, he got shelled. And that was the end of his pitching.

"Dad also told us about playing on a tennis team at a city college in Chicago. They placed him as the worst player against the worst player, and he went on to beat their best player. Dad had tremendous will. He also saw the Australian grand slam star champion Rod Laver and played tennis on the court next to him.

"We'd play Scrabble in his last days," Jackie adds. "It was how Dad escaped the pain. That's also how he ran our poker games. He could focus out the rest of the world when he was competing."

"We had a wonderful active last few months with him. Dad was so proud of each one of us." The room expands with love as Tommy speaks—a love that binds family and friends through the divinity within our hearts. "When his father died, Dad left college so he could go to work to care for his mother because he was the only child still living at home. That's why he wasn't able to become a doctor as he'd wished. Bubbi Dora died in 1967."

Next comes a moment of personal sweetness for me. Sara plays a five-minute video clip of Dad recounting two of his best stories: the atom bomb test and how as a child he almost died from convulsions. *The Divine Parent fulfilling my longing to immortalize my father's stories.* His voice and his smile on video—forever.

With the grace of an athelete, Brother Jackie articulates Dad's soul nature through the sport of tennis—the soul according to yogic doctrine defined as the individualized expression of Spirit.

"Who remembers Dad on the tennis courts?" Jackie begins. "His sense of knowing how to end a point was incredibly precise. He beat many players in mixed doubles who were much better than him as a singles player. Those were the guys who hit the textbook-pretty shots. But Zeke always landed the ball where the champions knew it belonged.

"When I was little, I watched him play with a windmill serve and no bend in his elbow. You remember that, Tommy Boy? Probably not. You were *way* too little yourself back then! Dad hit his forehand like he was holding a sock puppet, not a tennis racket. He would hold the racket close to his face. He hit his backhand with a barely modified forehand grip, causing his arm muscles to overcompensate with too little help from his body. What he forfeited in power and leverage, he made up for with a confident and relentless attack game. He poached often, putting the ball exactly where the opposing players weren't, or where they had little or no chance to capitalize. Oh, he knew how to end a point!

"Every shot in Dad's game was wrong. His forehand, backhand, serve, and volley were all examples of how *not* to hit a tennis ball."

My brother pauses.

A hush. A whisper. Dad is about to swing his racket.

"Yet six out of seven times, he would be the one putting the ball away."

THE FIRST *Yartzheit* FLAME

Wednesday, *September 2, 2009*
        Dear Dad,

The Jewish calendar differs from the traditional chronicling of time as you well know, and so tonight being the one-year anniversary of your passing and the cycling of four seasons without you, I lit the first yartzheit candle in remembrance of you, as I will for the rest of my life. Five candle flames will burn each year as long as there are five children to light them.

In honor of your request that the family stay close, I wrote to your sons: "You are all in my heart on this special night of remembrance of Dad. It's amazing that the drama of his courageous passing is over, and how we've all rallied to find our own strength to live in this world without him. This has been Dad's first year in Heaven and our first year on our own."

I arranged an altar that I thought would please you—with a cutting from the plant you used to water, the pipe with the plastic mouthpiece that you chewed to a pulp, and the candle itself. The Los Angeles Times *sports section would've been there too if I'd had a copy of it on*

hand. A few of your pencil sketches on shirt cardboards also deco-
rated the altar. And let's not forget your food coupons! As a survivor
of The Great Depression, how you loved to save a quarter here and
a nickel there, matching grocery items to the coupons you clipped
so meticulously from the morning newspaper. Your Scrabble tiles in
the red velvet pouch—and the score from our last game that you
won with flying colors just a week before you passed—completed
the altar.

I lit the candle and repeated in Hebrew what little I knew of the
prayer, finishing in mid-sentence like running to the very edge of a
precipice only to halt just before toppling over the brink. Do you think
G-d will forgive me for muddling it so badly? The actual Kaddish,
Moshe explained to me earlier today, is meant to be said only by men
at synagogue. Death and dying are not mentioned, which he said
makes it hard to understand this prayer's relationship to the deceased.
Judaic scripture declares that for one year after death, a person's soul
and his actions on earth are judged by Hashem.

This transition called death is explained differently by yogic
teachings: that the soul, still bound to an ego yet freed from the
shackles of the physical body, moves forward in its journey to God.
After a brief respite in the astral world, the soul with any remaining
unfulfilled desires returns to a body and to this world, until at last it
attains Self-realization.

Dad: Lighting this first yartzheit for you pierces my heart. I've
lit candles with you in times past—for Shabot, for high holidays, for
your parents, for Mom—but not for you. You never played easy with
me, neither in checkers nor in any part of our historic relationship.

Lighting this candle, father mine, is the hardest game of all.

I'd like to wax poetic and say that I see you in the loud colors of the setting sun and hear you in the soft textures of the brisk wind. Instead I feel you at the mall and hear you on the tennis courts. In the frozen foods section of the grocery store, I can almost see your shadow standing reverentially before the altar of discounted entrees in the towering glass freezers.

I see you in your sons and in their children and grandchildren.

And I see you in my heart.

At any restaurant I visit, I assume the waitress must be a personal friend of yours. Before I sit down to order from the menu, it's as though we already know each other. You've shown your children that everyone, no matter what their lot in life, has a song, a dance, a story.

Do you remember Joanne Barker, the financial director at the oncologist's office, how she broke down crying when she first met you? "For fifteen years I've worked here," she said, "and no one, Zeke, has ever once asked about my life and my children."

And guess what? Hardly a day goes by that I don't wear something you bought for me on one of our shopping trips.

If I might share this song with you from my spiritual community, the lyrics are so appropriate for this first yartzheit. We sing it when our friends leave for a trip or when guests are on their way home from a spiritual retreat. It represents the transition from what has come before to what transpires after.

Go with love, may joyful blessings
Speed you safely on your way.
May God's love expand within you:
May we be One in that light someday. [11]

Well, that's that. Maybe we didn't have a perfect charmed relationship.
Dysfunction-schmunction, whaddaya talkin' about? Life and death
are all about love. Father mine, go with love.

My spiritual practices have sustained me well through the passing of my father. Meditation, it is said, is a preparation for death. I've always thought the death of a loved one is one of the harshest tests we can endure in this world. Why? Because it triggers the unimaginably deeper grief of our separation from God—that we have lost at least temporarily the remembrance of our oneness with our One Parent. As all true religions and spiritual paths proclaim, there is ultimately and gloriously no separation between ourselves and the Divinity that lies within us.

May we be One in that realization.

THE END

EPILOGUE

Lila continues to embrace her path of yoga in the Ananda communities, spreading Spirit-in-Nature Essences worldwide. Her life burns steadily like candles on the Jewish Sabbath and on her meditation altar.

Phil, according to his sister, is one of the best doctors in the world. Scattered across his driveway is a hodgepodge of vintage cars, including his cherished 1920s British cab. He can still fix anything.

Jack has maintained his washboard abs and may donate them to charity or to the local laundromat. He's brainstorming a successful ad career, among other projects. And he Skypes regularly with his sister.

Moshe's organizations continue to bring vast numbers of young people back to the heart of Judaism. To sit at his Sabbath table is a profound blessing. And he's got at least a bazillion grandchildren. So, *nu?*

Tommy Boy has built a successful law firm overlooking the Pacific Ocean—much as he oversees his kids' practice sessions and tournaments for whatever they choose to excel in at the time.

Aaron Oscar (Zeke) is probably giving them hell in Heaven— calling everyone by their first name and winning at every possible astral game. Game-schmame, whaddaya talkin' about? Unless he has already reincarnated so he can continue to "do a good job."

Footnotes

1. Page 41, Yogananda, Paramhansa, *Cosmic Chants*, Self-Realization Fellowship, Los Angeles, CA., 1974.

2. Page 52, Walters, J. Donald, and Mukti, "O Master," Joyful Arts Production Association (BMI), Nevada City, CA, 2014.

3. Page 111, Walters, J. Donald, *The New Path*, Crystal Clarity Publications, Nevada City, CA, 1977, p. 454.

4. Page 183, Swami Kriyananda, *The Essence of the Bhagavad Gita*, Crystal Clarity Publishers, Nevada City, CA, 2006, p.102.

5. Page 196, Walters, J. Donald, *Rays of the One Light*, Crystal Clarity Publishers, Nevada City, CA, 1996, p. 13.

6. Page 199, Walters, J. Donald, "Life is A Dream," Joyful Arts Production Association (BMI), Nevada City, CA, 1990.

7. Page 244, Walters, J. Donald, *Living Wisely, Living Well*, Crystal Clarity Publishers, Nevada City, CA, 2010, p. 53.

8. Page 245, Kriyananda, Swami, *Revelations of Christ*, Crystal Clarity Publishers, Nevada City, CA, 2007, p. 427.

9. Page 242, Yogananda, Paramhansa, *Whispers from Eternity*, Crystal Clarity Publishers, Nevada City, CA, 2008, p. 134.

10. Page 291, Walters, J. Donald, "Home is a Green Hill," Ananda Church of Self-Realization, Nevada City, CA, 1998, p. 295.

11. Page 324, Walters, J. Donald, "Go With Love," Ananda Church of Self-Realization, Nevada City, CA, 2002.

GLOSSARY OF JEWISH/YIDDISH TERMS

Bar mitzvah: The rite of passage ceremony when a boy becomes a man at age thirteen, according to Jewish law.

Bris: Circumcision, a ceremony celebrating the birth of a Jewish boy.

Bubbi: Grandmother.

Chametz: Leavened food, unsuitable for the holiday of Passover.

Chutzpah: Brazenness, gall, nerve (slang).

Hashem: Hebrew word for Lord or God.

Kaddish: Memorial prayer for the dead by a mourner.

Kariya: The rending of clothing of mourners.

Kibitz: Chitchat; joking; also giving unwanted advice.

Kiddush: A Sabbath holiday blessing accompanied by the drinking of wine.

Keinayinhora: Good luck without the "evil eye," and that sometimes, it's better to hide one's fortune from others for fear of losing it.

Kvetch/kvetchie: Complain/complaining, whine.

Megillah: A long story, "the whole nine yards."

Mensch: An upstanding, honorable man who is worthy of respect.

Meshugenah: Crazy, nuts.

Minyan: A minimum of ten Jewish adults—specifically men in the orthodoxy—required for, most commonly, public prayer.

Mishugas: Craziness, nonsense, absurdity; eccentricity.

Mitzvah: Good deed.

Nosh: Snack.

Nichum Aveilim: Paying a *shiva* call; an act of kindness to those who have lost a loved one.

Nu?: So? Well?

Oygevalt: Woe is me.

Oygottenyu: Oh, God!

Oy vey izmir: Oh, woe is me.

Schlep: To carry, drag, lug; or a lazy person.

Schlimazel: Luckless person, one who has perpetual bad luck.

Schmaltz: Literally, chicken fat, or excessively sentimental, corny.

Schpilkes: Pins and needles, ants in one's pants, nervousness.

Seder: Ceremony at Passover, a high Jewish holiday.

Shabbot/Shabbat/Sabbath/Shabbas: A full day of rest and worship, beginning at sundown every Friday until sundown on Saturday.

Simchas hachayim: The expression of a joyous heart.

Sitting shiva: The tradition of mourning the loss of a loved one for seven days after his passing

Tzitzit: The fringe of a prayer shawl/*tallis* worn as an undergarment by orthodox men to feel engulfed by God and surrounded by the commandments.

Traif: Non-kosher, as in foods.

Tzimmes: To make a fuss or uproar; also a baked main dish of carrots, sweet potatoes, and sometimes beef.

Yartzheit: A candle lit yearly on the anniversary of a parent's passing.

Zayde: Grandfather.

Glossary of Yogic Terms

Devi: Spiritual name meaning Divine Mother, or "shining one."

Durga: One of the spiritual names for the Divine Mother. Two of Durga's qualities are non-attachment and generosity.

Gyanamata: Literally, "mother of wisdom."

Jyotish: Spiritual name meaning "inner light."

Karma: The sum total of every action, activity and thought we've ever had in this and every other lifetime.

Krishnadas: Spiritual name, meaning "servant, or devoted to, Krishna, in all forms."

Liladevi: Spiritual name meaning, literally, "goddess of the cosmic drama."

Mantradevi: Spiritual name meaning, "the repetition of Divine Mother's love."

Naidhruva: Spiritual name meaning "close to perfection."

Nalini: Spiritual name meaning "lotus, a flower which is a symbol of illumination and detachment, since it rises above the mud of its origins."

Paramhansa Yogananda: Paramhansa means "great swan," the swan symbolically able to separate milk from water; Yogananda means "bliss through yoga, or union with."

Prakash: Indian name meaning "light."

Reincarnation: The need to pass from one lifetime to another, in order to work out our accrued karma.

Sadhana: Spiritual practices of a truth seeker, often including yoga and meditation.

Sahaja: Indian name meaning "natural, disciplined, of right action."

Satsang: Spiritual companionship, fellowship with like-minded truth seekers.

Savitri: Spiritual name meaning, "loyalty to God, though typically a woman's loyalty to her husband."

Seva: Spiritual name meaning "service."

Soul: The individualized expression of God or Spirit.

Sudarshan: Spiritual name meaning "seeing beauty."

Swamiji: "One with the Self," also a teacher. "Ji" is a suffix denoting respect and reverence.

Vrittis: Karmic seed that lay dormant in the astral spine.

Yoga: Literally, union, most often with one's Higher Self.

About the Author

Lila Devi (*lee-lah day-vee*) has always had a romance with words and began writing her first novel, songs, and poetry in grade school. She looks for stories waiting to be written or simply enjoyed in the moment—a quality modeled by her father—and views life as a work of fiction with a recurring theme of developing higher consciousness. With a passable command of the English language, she's now focusing on Italian and prefers to stay mainly in the present tense. Halloween is her favorite holiday when she plays "the world's most authentic fake gypsy palm reader," astounding the children who visit her booth with her infallible inaccuracy.

Lila received a Bachelor of Arts degree with honors in English, psychology, and a secondary teaching certificate from the University of Michigan; founded Spirit-in-Nature Essences in 1977, the oldest flower essence company outside England (Spirit-in-Nature.com); authored several books, and has lived at the Ananda communities worldwide forever. Lila resides within view of the Umbrian sunsets outside Assisi, Italy, and regularly visits California. She loves a good bagel and has developed a taste for curry.